Smoke Stories

By Mike Davis

Tales of
a volunteer
firefighter

MORNING STAR PRESS

Smoke Stories:
Tales of a Volunteer Firefighter

Printed in the United States of America

Summary: A volunteer firefighter experiences humorous and sobering episodes from which he draws life lessons and spiritual truths.

Library of Congress Cataloging-in-Publication Data
Davis, Mike

Smoke Stories: Tales of a Volunteer Firefighter / Mike Davis – First Edition

ISBN: 978-0-9799918-0-6

1. Firefighters 2. Small towns 3. Michigan
I. Davis, Mike II. Title

Library of Congress Control Number: 2007943421

MORNING STAR PRESS

2682 Long Meadow Lane, Rochester Hills, MI 48307
www.morning-star-press.com
(248) 852-5485

To my parents
Kenneth and Mary Davis

My wife
June Kaye

My children
Christine and Jeffrey

You have always laughed with me and I have
appreciated the love that went with the humor.

A portion of the proceeds of this book will go to a
fireman's Goodfellows fund.

I can think of no more stirring symbol of man's
humanity to man than a fire engine.

- Kurt Vonnegut

Smoke Stories

By Mike Davis

Tales of
a volunteer
firefighter

Table of Contents

CHAPTER 1

How It All Started

As long as I could remember, when people asked what I wanted to be when I grew up, my answer was usually, "A policeman or fireman." My grandfather was the local township supervisor, and to my everlasting delight every December he arranged for me to ride on the back of the fire truck during our hometown Christmas parade. After one of these rides, I somehow became a hero when I returned to my fourth grade class at school. Being a fireman and being cool seemed to go hand-in-hand.

My plans all changed when I went to high school and a favorite teacher talked me into studying for a career in graphic arts. Later, a college professor recommended me to a college of education, which enabled me to combine education with my technical knowledge in graphic arts. My dreams of being a police officer or firefighter began to fade, although I continued to follow the yearly reports of employment needs in our state for the police and fire service.

Four months after I graduated from college, my plans were shifted for me. I was drafted into the United States Army. When I inquired about the possibility of fire or police work in the Army, it turned out they were more than willing to assign me to a military police unit. But to do that, I would have to extend my two-year draft status to a four-year enlistment. The commanding officers said that with my degree and desire, I would do well as an officer with the military police.

I had a decision to make. Although I did not fight the fact that I was drafted, I did not wish to add years to my military obligation. I'd already married and had a young child before being drafted, and being away from them was not my idea of a family life. So I decided against the military police assignment, and was designated as a classification and interview specialist instead.

My task was to assign each recruit a military job based on his civilian experiences and training. I was one in a unit of nine people responsible for doling out the military job assignments. If a soldier had already been assigned a job at enlistment, then I simply made sure the paperwork was in order for that assignment. This was an interesting position for a draftee like me because it required a dress uniform every day and I got to interview some very interesting people. Some of the recruits were so naïve they thought they had crossed the ocean to get to Fort Knox. It was up to me to break the news to them that it was the Ohio River, not the Atlantic Ocean, that they had flown over.

Toward the end of my Army obligation, the United States was pulling out of Vietnam. Many people were leaving the military and often ended up in unemployment lines upon their return to the United States. At that time, early releases were allowed if a soldier returned to college full time or had a guaranteed job when discharged. So I decided to apply for an early release as well. I was granted a two-month early release and used my education and military experience to enroll in a university student teaching internship program. At the end of the experience, the teacher I was working under (who had been my high school teacher) retired. I was offered his job and the dream of being a firefighter or police officer appeared to be fading even further away.

When the internship was completed, my wife June, our four-year-old daughter Christy, and I moved into a small house on a lake about twenty miles from our hometown of Meadowbrook. I had married my high school sweetheart and we wanted to live near our parents. I'd had a wonderful relationship with my grandparents and we wanted the same for our children. June and I did all our socializing with old friends from the hometown and did not rule out moving back to Meadowbrook in the future.

Meadowbrook was a small town that never seemed to grow or die. It had a blinker light that became a true stop light as traffic increased from surrounding areas. The main street included the firehouse, a hardware store, a party store, a pizza shop, a tire store, a doctor's office, a bank, a barbershop, and a beauty salon. The post office was just a block out of town near the gas station. A small river and railroad track made Meadowbrook a typical all-American small town. The only thing that would cause any change in the architectural features along this street was rebuilding after a fire. My grandfather, who owned the local grocery store (now the party store), would answer his phone saying, "Davis' Friendly Market, Mr. Friendly speaking!" The usual Memorial Day parade, starting at the Legion Hall and ending at the Mom's Monument, also made Meadowbrook a typical small town.

But all that was twenty miles away one hot summer Sunday afternoon, when my wife and I invited many of our young friends and families for a day on the lake at our home. It was a large group with plenty of kids and hot dogs. We water-skied, took rides on the pontoon boat, and in general just enjoyed the waterfront. As the sun began to show red and orange colors in the sky, everyone gathered on the lawn. The kids were petting the dogs and the men were talking about men stuff and the women were talking about men and their stuff, too. In the conversation of stories, my almost-faded dream started to show signs of coming back to stark reality. My friend Vinny offered me the opportunity to join the fire department as a paid on-call firefighter if we ever moved back to the old hometown. Many of my friends were firefighters with Vinny and the idea seemed wonderful. But it also seemed impossible because we lived so far away.

Vinny was about ten years older than me. He was a dispatcher for a local cement company and worked just a block away from the firehouse. He was available at all hours to respond to calls and therefore was assigned to the post of assistant chief for station number one. The Meadowbrook fire department had a full time chief and three part time assistant chiefs for each of the three stations. Vinny and his family attended many of the same social functions and church activities as did our family, and we were good friends. As inviting as his offer was, however, it still seemed very far away.

Then two years later, it happened. A beautiful ranch house

in Meadowbrook just a few blocks from the fire station became available. It would be just five miles from my work and would put us closer to our friends and family. It seemed terribly expensive at the time, taking every last dollar we could find as well as a little help from our folks.

We bought the house and we were back in Meadowbrook near family and grandparents for our kids. It was great to walk into businesses and be called by name, particularly for me, a third generation in the area. Vinny, true to his word, had me on the fire department in just a couple of months.

My dream of being a firefighter had finally come true. As the new rookie on the department at station number one, I was proud. However, those first few months as a rookie let me in for a truckload of harassment. If it was broken, I was blamed for breaking it. If it was lost, I was faulted for losing it. If the pot was empty, it was my job to make more rich, black coffee. Never mind that some of those mugs in the cupboard looked like all you had to do was add water and the crust would make its own coffee.

But I took it all in stride as my longtime dream of becoming a firefighter had finally been realized. However, it was not long before another fine young man joined our distinguished group of smoke eaters and I polished my title of "rookie" and passed it on with a smile.

After Glow

It's funny how things just seem to work out: the un-expected change of career plans, the sudden military obligation, and the surprising move back to Meadow-brook. God had a plan. And if I had not been open to His plan, I may have ended up in a large city fire depart-ment, far from my hometown family and friends.

Seeking His plan always provides the best results for our particular needs. It is important to put forth the effort to improve your situation in life, but it is equally important to listen to the still small voice of our Heav-enly Father for His direction to true happiness and a life of fulfillment. In God's instruction book, the Bible, Proverbs 16:1-9 provides sound advice, especially verse 3: "Commit your work to the Lord and your plans will be successful."

CHAPTER 2

The First Fire

You might call it coincidence, but from the day I was officially put on the department roster until four weeks later, we did not get a single call. Of course, we had our usual weekly drills, but the guys were sure that I had been the one responsible for all previous fires and calls for medical assistance in the community because we were experiencing this rare period of mysterious quiet only since I joined. For that entire four-week period, the Plectron in my home was eerily silent. This was the one-way communication device we used at the time to alert firefighters of a call. I made sure to put it someplace where I could hear it throughout the house, but all it seemed to be doing was taking up a space about the size of two side-by-side shoeboxes. I eagerly awaited the tones the dispatcher would send to activate it and anticipated the contest all firefighters seemed to engage in to see if they could get dressed and out of the house before the dispatcher finished describing the incident and location.

The strange stillness came to a clanging end on a bitter January 20th at 5:00 in the morning. Because of the near-zero temperature, I took a few extra minutes to dress warmly. As a result, I lost the contest that morning, and hadn't yet made it out of the house before I heard the dispatcher say that there had been an explosion at the home of T.H. Florson. A chill went up my back that had nothing to do with the cold. In the short drive to the firehouse, I thought about T.H. Florson.

T.H. had been my eighth grade English teacher. He was from the old school with rigid rules and he possessed a huge nose. "The Nose," as my friends and I affectionately called him in private, took pride in preying on kids like me who were barely able to keep our grades floating above "C" level. To talk in his class was to ignite a wrath greater than anything that you may ever have read about in the Bible. He had a large sign over the clock in his classroom that read "Time will pass: will you?"

Further adorning this room of doom were two towels hanging on the wall near the door. One was rather long and was labeled "large crying towel." The other was a shorter towel and was labeled "small crying towel." As students, we spent several days developing the courage to ask for an audience with The Nose concerning a grade. But that was not what he expected out of his students. Once, when I finally forced myself to throw myself at his mercy, he simply pointed toward the towels to take care of my troubles. When I indicated to the man that I was not going to be popular among my siblings and parents when I took the grade home, the nose on his face got so red that I knew if I stayed, I might see the devil himself. I passed up the crying towel and decided the clock was quiet and time was passing so I was going to do the same.

Mrs. Florson, on the other hand, was an elementary teacher who was the model of all teachers. The direct opposite of her husband, Mrs. Florson had a caring demeanor, a love of children, and a kind voice that made school fun. My wife had the pleasure of having Mrs. Florson and she loved her class. Her teacher floated around the classroom like an angel even though she was a bit heavy.

Mrs. Florson could have been a doctor, as she knew the location of bones perfectly. If one of the boys in the class did not flow with the others in the beautiful happy activities of the classroom, his collar bone was unerringly located by Mrs. Florson's thumb and forefinger, which gently but firmly showed the unfortunate miscreant the path to righteousness. The devil would never have had a chance in her classroom of paradise. I have since known children who did not want to go home because her classroom was safer than their home.

So here I was responding to old Florson's house some twelve years later. The Nose was retired and I was a teacher and volunteer (paid on-call) firefighter. I was on the tailboard of a 1250 pumper, half dressed, cold, and scared to death of meeting my first house fire. My partner on the tailboard was my church pastor, Rev. Cypress. I respected Rev. Cypress as a precise and thorough man. His attention to detail and polished appearance was exactly what I needed as I responded to this call as a rookie. When we rolled up on the scene of this explosion, the preacher's presence did not allow me to say what I was thinking in exactly the words I wanted to. However, as time went on, I began to wish fervently that I had used the restroom before responding to this call. It took several hours to extinguish the flames as natural gas kept feeding the fire. This was a tight neighborhood so we worked hard to protect the perimeter and save the other homes.

Ironically, the Florsons did not have natural gas in their home. It was determined later that the frost was so deep into the ground that a gas leak somewhere in the ground followed the city water line to their basement. When their oil furnace activated, the gas-filled basement exploded and the home was destroyed. Both Mr. and Mrs. Florson survived. There were several small explosions near the sidewalk as the gas was leaking all through the ground. It was a very hair-raising couple of hours, especially for me, the rookie, a term I used heavily that day. The Florsons were protected by their bed and walked away with minor burns, but lost everything in the blast, and had to start over from clothes to dishes. They said the pictures were the hardest to lose.

My wife and I gave the Florsons a gift after the fire had destroyed their home. They were housed in an apartment while their house was being rebuilt. The entire community showered them with gifts that helped them until the insurance company sent them their check. Our gift was a new automatic coffee maker, but it seemed my fate to mess that up, too. The day after we delivered the coffee maker to the Florsons, our local paper ran a front page report about how the coffee maker that we gave them was being recalled because it might cause a fire if unattended. I bet the old Nose got red on that one!

A few years later, old T.H. Florson died. Mrs. Florson asked if I would speak at the funeral of The Nose. What on earth was I going to say? The man scared me so much that I used to flip our dog's dish each night before feeding her to see how it landed. If it landed right side up, it meant a good day in The Nose's class, and we may even get a substitute. Of course, as it ended up, there never were any substitutes. I didn't even want to imagine The Nose with a cold. If the dish landed upside down, that meant I would read the Bible a bit longer that night. The Nose made me a religious person, but not a very healthy person. I threw up in his class before the year ended. I told the group at the small funeral that many of my teachers influenced my teaching style. I put to use the good ideas and filtered out the bad methods. Enough said!

After Glow

It's strange how some people influence your life. While going to English class in the eighth grade, I could not imagine how anything T.H. Florson was doing could help me in the future. Little did I know that one day I would be a teacher and would have to develop my own style of methods for the classroom. My experience in T.H. Florson's class was always in the back of my mind when I saw a student struggling. I worked hard to provide an open, resourceful classroom.

God used T.H. Florson to influence me just as he used Paul in the New Testament. In Galatians 1:11-24, Paul (the one who persecuted Christians) was later used as one of the most influential people in the history of Christianity. He ended up molding and providing guidance to the early church. Sometimes when we find ourselves in a bad situation, we discover later that it allowed us to grow and mature for the greater work ahead.

CHAPTER 3

My Best Buddy Buck

My best friend Buck was also a fellow firefighter. People told us that we looked a lot alike. I was a little taller and Buck was a little heavier and stronger. We hunted and fished together, cut firewood with our boys for fun, and trusted our families to each other. He was an excellent stone mason, a trade that he learned from his father. His sons have also developed the talent as well. Buck was great at anything with his hands; he was a talented person and a good fireman.

As paid on-call volunteer firefighters, we responded in our personal vehicles to the fire hall. Our pick-ups and cars were equipped with beacon lights and sirens. As I look back on the experience, we were real cowboys on the road when the fire whistle went off in town. The entire town could hear the whistle, so people pulled off the road as firefighters came out of the side streets to get to the fire hall.

When Buck and I responded to the fire hall, we usually either positioned ourselves to be partners on the tailboard, or I would drive and he would take the passenger seat, or the shotgun position, as we called it. We were a team and didn't even need to talk when we got into a hot situation. Each of us simply knew what the other would do and we depended on that relationship, sometimes for our very lives.

We each had our weaknesses, and the other compensated for them. For instance, on medical runs, Buck handled vomit and I handled blood. On horrible fires, he did the cussing and I did the screaming. On cardio-pulmonary resuscitation (CPR) runs, our methods saved the lives of several people. Our mutual friend, Assistant Chief Vinny, covered our butts more than once when our antics turned toward the somewhat unprofessional as reported by Captain Norman Scott.

One such unprofessional act occurred during a smoke investigation call at a drug store. When we arrived, an arrogant driver of an expensive sports car left his vehicle parked at the door of the drug store in the fire lane. The windows were down and it appeared that the driver was the type of person to whom the rules and signs did not apply. He was apparently better than the rest of us regular folks who followed the rules. Buck pulled an inch-and-a-half pre-connected hose line from the fire truck and ran it through the windows of the sports car and into the store. I charged the line with water right about the time the hotshot stranger from out of town came out of the store. He asked me what the @#%* I thought I was doing, and the police officer behind me asked the hotshot the same question. It took us most of an hour to find the cause of the smoke. That left plenty of time for the cop to write the $75 ticket.

▼

For several years I had been traveling to a mountain mission in Kentucky to distribute used clothing from our church. Every four or five months I loaded up my truck and trailer and found a friend to travel with me to help unload at the mission. I took Buck on one of those trips. He had never traveled out of state, so the experience was all new to him. Buck did not have much use for organized religion, but later, after some discussion, he did join our small church.

Before the trip, I told Buck that we would be meeting a local mission coordinator named Stick. I can't remember anyone saying his last name or even a first name if Stick was his last name. Everybody just called him Uncle Stick. Anyway, I told Buck that Uncle Stick was hard of hearing and that he would have to speak loudly for the old man to understand him. When we arrived, I was able to get to Uncle Stick first and told him about my friend Buck who was hard of hearing, Buck and Stick, of course, both had excellent hearing but they yelled at each other the entire weekend. By Sunday, I too was hard of hearing.

▼

Buck and I fought a lot of fires and one of our pastimes was cutting firewood. We packed up the pickup truck with a chain saw and our sons, trying to make men out of the boys. Later, my son Jeff said testosterone and seeing a chain saw next to a dead oak tree made him feel like a man. Jeff is now married and has a son of his own, so his philosophy may have changed in the last year or so.

On one of our wood cutting trips, I saw a huge vine hanging in the woods from some trees. The vine was so thick that it could be cut with a chain saw. I was swinging on the thing showing off and pretty soon all the others joined in on the fun. Two days later I began to break out in what turned out to be a poison oak rash.

That afternoon we got a fire call and again Buck and I were on the tailboard of the fire truck. It was fun, riding on the back of the truck in those days – no safety harness, smelling the exhaust of the truck, siren wailing, red lights flashing, and flying through town. While we were heading toward the run, I told Buck that I got a pretty bad case of poison oak over the weekend. He laughed uproariously at that, but it turned out there was plenty of embarrassment to go around. It turned out Buck had drunk too much pop that day and had to answer a call of nature that I hadn't had to. He said that the resulting swelling had been rather embarrassing, so he decided his son needed to carry toilet paper the next time we went woodcutting. After all, using poison oak in a portion of the anatomy where toilet paper is generally used is very painful.

After Glow

The poison oak experience turned out to be an uncomfortable ordeal that required patience and medication. It was an experience that changed how we approached oak trees forever after that. Poison oak grows around those stately oaks and is as strong as a farmer's rope. The effect on humans varies with each person. Every one of us who came in contact with the stuff had a reaction to that vine except for my son. He was completely unaffected.

People are a lot like that as well. A negative person at work can get on the nerves of just about everyone. But there is inevitably one person that the negativity simply does not affect. When you ask people like that how they can ignore such negativity they reply something like, "Nobody can shadow me with negativity unless I let them. I have control of what affects me and I choose not to let that person's negativity bother me and I use forgiveness." People like that impress me like the heaping coals story in Romans 12:19-21. They prove that the best way to conquer evil is by doing good.

CHAPTER 4

Lurch, Shaky, and Willy Tan

In our community, there were three fire stations. Each of the stations usually had twenty members on the roster. All the members had full-time jobs, and being a paid on-call volunteer was just a service that we did for the community. Of the twenty members at each station, ten were employed in the daytime and ten worked night-shift jobs. This allowed for people to be available both night and day to respond to medical and fire-related calls.

I introduced one of my neighbors, Jake Sea, to our Station Number One members. He was a big man and looked and acted like Lurch on *The Addams Family*. He even sounded like Lurch and you could tell he was a 1970's recycled hippie. I liked the guy, but he and Buck, my best friend, did not get along very well at all.

During a winter storm one day, we were on standby at the fire station. Often the chief would ask a few of us to man the station during such storms in order to have better response times. Some of us used our four-wheel-drive personal vehicles or snowmobiles and others drove all-terrain vehicles when the weather required such responses. During such storms, we had a lot of elderly folks who often lost their power and they depended on us to pump basements when a sump pump did not have electricity. Often, we had to transport folks to the fire hall where our generator kept the heat and lights working and we warmed a big pot of chili made by our wives. I always hated to see Buck eat the chili, that smile on his face when he did so made me sick.

During this particular storm, Buck, Jake Sea (Lurch), and I were on duty with several others on a cold, late night fire station standby. After finishing a few chores around the station, we were playing cards near the coffeepot.

As volunteers, we did not have work uniforms. We usually had blue jeans and sweatshirts and baseball caps on until we got a call. There was kind of a code at the fire hall. No long hair and nothing but baseball caps or hunting hats could be worn, just men stuff. Our fire coats and pants and helmets all fit over our regular clothes.

In the middle of the card game, Buck asked Lurch where he got the stupid-looking stocking hat that he was wearing. Lurch said his wife had knitted it, but I had to admit that it looked stupid and I told him I had to agree with Buck. Buck said that, with all of those pastel colors, it looked like someone had puked on his head.

Well, that did it. Lurch stood up as if to take issue with Buck, and man, he was big. Just then we got a call and our attention was turned to the medical emergency.

When we returned, I figured the hat incident was over, but when we hung up our helmets and coats, Lurch's puke hat was missing. It seemed everybody thought that that puke hat made the department look stupid. I sure do not know why, but Lurch continued to wear that hat even after he found it dipped in water and frozen to the aerial of his car that night. Lurch didn't last very long and he resigned before the year's probation was over. It was too bad; we really needed a big man to knock down doors on really big fires, but I think one way or another that hat clouded his thinking.

▼

We had a few cadets in our department. They were teenagers who hoped to be a part of our program one day. They were not allowed to respond to the station with lights and siren. They usually arrived after the truck had pulled out and busied themselves with the hall maintenance. When the truck returned, they helped roll hoses and hang wet hoses in the hose tower to dry.

When any one of them climbed the ladder inside the hose tower, he was just twelve inches from the community siren. Every evening at 6:00, the siren automatically went through one cycle. Some communities had a noon whistle, but in our town, it was the 6:00 PM whistle that got you home for dinner. We sure enjoyed getting some unsuspecting cadet up in the tower a few minutes before the 6:00 PM blast of the siren. After the experience, the poor kid would talk really loud for some thirty minutes because of his impaired hearing.

We sometimes allowed the cadets to come to the scene of a fire to help with cleanup after the fire was extinguished. We used the experience to explain how we attacked the fire and in general showed them how tough we were.

One of the cadets we called Shaky. He drummed on everything during our weekly drills. He fidgeted during meetings and was a bundle of nerves. He was a really nice kid and smart, too; in fact I recommended him for lieutenant some years later. Willy Tan, one of our longtime members, gave Shaky his nickname after the cadet rattled Willy's chair during a fire association meeting.

Willy Tan was a really nice guy, but he refused to drive the fire truck and was very nervous when talking on the radio. He was usually the first to respond to the fire hall. He was an excellent backup man and when someone did something stupid, he was the first to signal the warning that the wrongdoer was doing something dumb. Shaky, on the other hand, never sat in a chair, that was too confining. He must have been a real case for his teachers at the local high school. The old metal folding chairs that we used for the meetings were in really bad shape and there were not enough to go around. On one of our drill nights, Shaky was fidgeting so badly on the rung of Willy Tan's chair, it caused the chair to collapse. Willy was a bit overweight and was usually showing cleavage above his jeans about his buttocks area. That night when the chair collapsed, the only way we could tell which end of Willy was up was by the scar on his head. All we saw was bald head and bare butt at various intervals. The scar on his head was from falling off the fire truck and he did that all by himself without Shaky. Shaky was a star that night, but Willy was seeing stars. It usually was a disaster when the two of them were together, and this night was no exception.

But the night finally came when Willy pulled one on Shaky. The first and third Wednesdays of each month, we had to attend a drill at the fire hall. On drill night, we taught rookies and cadets the ropes and practiced operating the fire trucks or walking through new buildings. This helped us get oriented for hydrant location and other water supplies. We also recorded where power sources to the building were and noted other areas likely to need our attention during an emergency. On really cold nights, we simply sat in a circle on those old flimsy chairs and drew street addresses from a coffee can and described how we would get to that location with a fire truck.

On this particular drill night, we were studying hose lines inside the fire hall. We put on our full gear, including breathing tanks and masks. The mask was blacked out to simulate a smoke-filled room at night. The one in training had to feel the hose to find his way out of the room, crawling on the floor over several mixed hose lines. He had to learn how to identify, blind, which line was his, and from the coupling, determine which way was out of the fire and which way put him back into the dangerous fire at the nozzle.

Well, this was Willy's night to shine. He set up Shaky through a maze of scrambled hose lines that led through the aforementioned broken chair. Finally, Shaky, loaded with gear and a mask that was blacked out, worked his way to the end of the line, out of danger. As he reached the end of the hose to the water source, his glove filled up with water. Seemed that Shaky's hose somehow ended in the public toilet. Shaky was a good sport about it, but he began walking wide circles around Willy.

I remember a couple of years before the chair incident, Willy was riding on the tailboard with one of his buddies by the name of Woolwood. Buck and I were in the cab of the fire truck. Buck was handling the maps and I drove the truck and responded on the radio. Woolwood was also a pretty heavy man and often wore sweatpants to the calls because they were easy to put on in the night and seemed to be warm. Before we had the heavy pants and coats, we simply wore rubber raincoats and hip-high rubber boots. It was during this time that Woolwood responded in his truck to the fire hall, grabbed his boots, coat, and helmet, and was on the tailboard in a flash. This was not an easy thing for a man of about 245 pounds.

It was important to hurry because the first five guys in the fire hall got to ride the truck and respond to the call. The others would have to stay at the hall and mop the floors and do general maintenance unless the assistant chief called for another truck. The assistant chief always arrived at the scene first because he responded directly to the address from his home. He also had a walkie-talkie so that he could talk to the dispatcher, the responding truck, and the fire hall.

On this particular night, the 245-pound Woolwood was pulling the string of his sweatpants to tighten them about his waist. I drove the truck over some railroad tracks and the bump jarred Woolwood so badly that he pulled the string completely out of his pants, leaving absolutely nothing to hold his pants up. The call turned out to be a working house fire and Woolwood was a lead hoseman, crawling on all fours, which created a few images that I will leave to the reader's imagination.

Reminds me of the story of the sled dogs. It seems that the lead dog is the only one who gets a change of scenery.

After Glow

We cross paths with a lot of different kinds of people in our work and leisure time. It is important to be patient and use maturity to understand what people are thinking and the reason for their decisions. Many times, the best way to influence people is to just be an example of your faith. Several years ago, there was a national awareness and concern about wearing items of jewelry that define our faith in the workplace. The president at the time was Gerald Ford, and he was asked his opinion on the issue. His response has impressed me for a long time. He simply told the group that he did not have to wear his faith, he just lived his faith. In I Thessalonians 1:8, Paul, the great New Testament preacher, tells the Thessalonian people that they are to be commended for living their faith to the point that he didn't have to preach in the area at all. Their remarkable faith was well known everywhere.

Wow, to have that kind of influence just by going about doing your job to the best of your ability with a genuine concern for others! The day will come when someone will surprise you and say, "I saw your example and have applied your idea in my life with wonderful

CHAPTER 5

More Response Calls With Buck

My favorite story about firefighting with Buck was the time that the two of us responded alone to a working house fire. The call came in just after midnight. I arrived at the fire hall in my pickup, meeting Buck at about the same time. A strange, almost eerie feeling came over us as no other firemen responded during those first critical minutes. As usual, I drove the 1250 pumper and Buck took shotgun.

There was no need to read a map for the address. As soon as the huge electric garage doors opened in front of the fire truck, we could see the flames of the house just half a block away. The house was an older two-story home that had been rented, but was currently vacant. The owner had several rental houses on that corner, one of which he occupied. We were always careful approaching empty and abandoned buildings since arson was always a possibility.

When we arrived, I engaged the pump of the truck so Buck could fight the fire with the five hundred gallons of water we carried on board. This gave me time to hook up to a fire hydrant next to which I had positioned the truck. Five hundred gallons sounds like a lot of water, but that amount of water will only last two or three minutes when the truck is capable of pumping 1,250 gallons a minute. It was imperative that I have the hydrant supplying the truck within a couple of minutes or Buck would be out of water and left in a dangerous position depending how far into the fire he had attacked. Once again, we depended on each other for our very lives. Buck and I were young, strong, quick, and in our minds, excellent firemen.

In a matter of minutes, Buck had knocked down the flames of the fire single-handedly, with the support of his driver/engineer: me. He put the nozzle down and turned to walk back to the truck, removing his mask and air tanks. A second truck was finally responding with other firefighters. Buck and I were high-fiving each other and he said, "Dang, we just put out a house fire with one truck and two awesome firemen."

Just then, the chief made his way to us. We thought he was coming to congratulate us for the quick response and strategic attack on the fire. But he busted the balloons of our vanity as he said that a lot of smoke was still coming from the roof vents. It was hard to see the smoke at night, but the chief was experienced and had a spotlight. And here we thought he was going to give us a pat on the back. But we thought we could handle smoky roof vents. All that changed in the next few seconds when the house exploded. The next minute, there I was getting religion with my buddy Buck, both of us talking out loud to God that night.

It was believed that the house fire was set on purpose. The suspected arsonist had placed several containers of fuel all through the abandoned house. Buck was lucky that he was away from the house when the second group exploded.

▼

The late-night domestic violence call was another story that Buck and I often reminisce about in our retirement. By this time, all the firefighters had the new modern voice pagers. The pagers allowed us to hear the status of the call and any new information as it was received. This was especially helpful for those of us on the back of the truck who were out of radio contact.

The request came through to respond to this call with medical equipment because of an injury as a result of the domestic violence. We were further directed to remain at the curb in the truck until the police cleared the scene of any danger. There was no problem following that request, those cops sure earn their money. The dispatcher said that the live-in boyfriend slammed a door on a young female's hand and she could not stop the bleeding. We were to provide immediate first aid as the ambulance was being delayed. Yeah, right. They were always delayed when they heard that the police had to clear the scene first.

The latest information we had was that the boyfriend had left the home in a rage. He was reported to be driving a pickup truck and had a loaded, muzzle-loading pistol in his possession. When we arrived, we were standing out in the street by the fire truck talking about what we would do to a guy who beat his girlfriend. About that time, a pickup came recklessly around the corner at the same time that one of our rookies slammed the door to the fire truck, which sounded like a pistol shot. Buck and I, both having had military experience, hit the dirt. We were quick and always knew what the other was thinking. Right about this time, I remembered that it was 2:00 AM and I should have been at home in bed. We were able to help the woman with the injured hand and fortunately never got to meet the boyfriend.

▼

And then there was the first car fire that I responded to with Buck. I was a rookie at the time and Assistant Chief Vinny wanted me to gain some live-action experience. Car fires and dumpster fires were usually routine in nature and provided excellent training for new firefighters. Someone had stolen an old station wagon and when they were finished joy riding around town, they set fire to it behind the high school. It was blazing pretty well when we arrived, and as ordered by Vinny, and under his watchful eye, I began my attack. Buck was my backup and I asked Vinny if the car was going to blow up. He said that it sure as hell would if I didn't get the fire out now!

Just as I approached the hot, blazing fire, I pulled the nozzle valve to my inch-and-a-half line and just as the water hit the flames, an explosion tore through the air. I thought I was dead and found myself on my knees thinking, "Why am I doing this? I am only a volunteer."

As I took inventory of myself, reassuring myself that I had all of my appendages, I also realized that it was only one of the tires that had exploded. My fellow brothers of the fire service were laughing so hard that I was sure that I would hear about this incident time and again in the future.

▼

Buck and I look a lot alike. I am taller, but some of our facial features are similar and we both have mustaches. Once, Buck was lost on a bay on one of the Great Lakes due to motor problems, and my face was used to show people what he looked like as we searched.

One late Sunday night, we received a medical call to the home of an elderly woman. Sunday evening medical calls to the homes of elderly people were fairly common, especially in the winter. This was usually true of folks living alone. A call to the dispatch of "difficulty breathing" would get these folks a house full of people and attention at no charge. We would check them over thoroughly and assure them that they were OK, but assure them that the ambulance would transport them to get "checked out" if they wished. They usually refused the ambulance, but appreciated our attention.

We had been called to this particular home on several occasions and usually on Sunday evenings. The older lady who lived here appeared very lonely and had several ongoing medical problems. She lived alone, but had relatives checking on her occasionally for groceries and medications. It only took a phone call to our dispatch to get five men in her bedroom in about eight minutes. When we arrived, we took her blood pressure and pulse, and completed a general first aid check.

I left the bedside to get an oxygen tank from the engine when Buck took over my routine medical check. When I returned with the oxygen tank, she looked at Buck and said, "I want you," and she pulled Buck onto her bed. Buck said, "No, the other guy is the one you want. He just looks like me." She was probably forty years our senior, but Buck looked good that night. That sure got her blood pressure up a bit. When the ambulance crew arrived, they determined that she was a bit feverish, slightly sweaty, and had an elevated blood pressure. It was decided that she should be transported to the hospital to be checked out thoroughly. That devil Buck, being a family man, said he would let a doctor put that fire out!

On another busy afternoon, we were called to respond to a medical emergency at the halfway house in our community. About ten people lived in this house with their caregivers. Each of the residents had a mental deficiency that required that they have some assistance in their living arrangements. Buck and I were on the tailboard again with our newly installed safety harnesses. New regulations required us to wear a safety harness when riding on the tailboard of the truck. That would later change to no tailboard riding at all. A colorful era would be gone.

The new pager allowed us to hear that this incident involved a woman who had fallen in the shower and was bleeding badly about the head and neck. Buck and I rushed into the house with our big orange first aid box and oxygen tank. As soon as we evaluated the situation, I asked Buck to give me a sanitary napkin from the orange box to control the bleeding on her neck and head. Buck does not do blood, so he was not looking when he handed me the item. The poor woman was naked except for a towel wrapped loosely around her body. Even someone with all mental faculties intact would have been alarmed to have five strange men working on her in that state of dress.

When Buck pulled that sanitary napkin package from the box, the woman bit Buck and said, "You're not putting that on me, you pubert!" I think she meant pervert, but the name stuck for a while. I even bought Buck a hat with his new name on the front. He finally grew out of the name sometime later after another experience.

A major interstate goes through our little town, and as a result, our department responded to numerous medical emergencies for car and truck mishaps. One unusual night, Buck and I found ourselves crawling under an overturned jack-knifed semi tractor-trailer. The truck was leaking diesel fuel all over the road. We were using a paste material called Dyke to patch the hole in the fuel tank through which the fuel was leaking. Dyke was a powdered material that, mixed with a small amount of water, made a pasty substance. It worked great on drill night with good lighting and plenty of time. But this night was dark and stopping that fuel tank leak was critical in keeping the highway from becoming slick with fuel oil and water. There was a lot of commotion at the scene and it was very dark. I was holding a portable light for Buck as he patched the hole when, all of a sudden, I heard a hissing sound. I said to Buck, or I should say I yelled to Buck, "Lets get out of here. I hear a hissing sound and I want to know where it is coming from before I stay any longer."

I don't remember what he said to me but he started laughing at me. I don't know what he was doing under there after I left, but whatever he was doing, he was doing it in the dark, because I was out of there with the portable light in my hand. Vinny told me that I was a chicken and that the hissing was the air brake lines leaking a little bit of air, but by that time, I didn't care. I was leaking air too.

▼

In the early 1980's, the majority of our calls were for medical response. One such response involved a head-on collision. The vehicles involved were a pickup truck and a small sports car. The truck had a front-mounted spare tire on a steel beam. It was a four-wheel-drive truck jacked up a bit for off-road driving. The sports car was a very small foreign two-seat model. To say the least, the sports car sustained a lot of damage and the driver was still trapped, unconscious, in the car. The driver of the pickup was running around angrily and wanted to blame everything and everyone for the delay this accident was causing him.

When we arrived at the scene, it was clear that the attention needed to be on the sports car driver. I worked hard to stabilize him and stop the heavy bleeding. We were in the middle of the road and traffic was brushing our coats trying to get by during rush hour. The police had not yet arrived. As usual in bloody situations, Buck was assisting me when he spotted a pearl-handled handgun lying on the road in the huge space under the four-wheel-drive pickup. There were a lot of people crowded around the accident but there was no one I recognized who could help us keep an eye on that pistol.

We were successful in bringing the sports car driver to

consciousness and we used a cervical collar to support his neck. Buck was working to tear off the door of the car so we could safely get the man out without further injury. All the while, we kept a nervous, watchful eye on the gun. Even if it was not loaded, we were sweating the bullets. To add to the difficulty, the driver of the truck wanted to fight the driver of the sports car because he came into the pickup driver's lane. There was also a racial issue and there were several racial slurs that the crowd was picking up on. The crowd did help keep the pickup driver away from our work until the police arrived.

The police carefully retrieved the handgun and brought it over to me. The officer asked me to look at the manufacturer of the gun, which read "Mattel." The smart aleck officer said, "Look, it's a Mattel! It's Swell!" That had been the slogan of the Mattel Toy Company in the old days.

After Glow

As firemen, we expect certain reactions to our procedures by the general public, but often the reactions are the opposite of our expectations. When an emergency vehicle is approaching from behind, it is the law to pull to the right side of the road. Whether it's a four-lane highway or a one-way street, that rule seems to confuse people as they will just as likely to go to the left side of the road as the right. As we grow older, we like to think that we have a greater understanding of things and their outcomes. We naturally use our experiences to project what we expect from a situation. Trouble is, we have been surprised before and we are fairly sure we will be surprised again.

Thank goodness that is not true of Jesus Christ. Hebrews 13:8 tells us that Christ is the same yesterday, today, and forever. When something is as solid as the promise of Jesus Christ, that foundation will stand the test of time forever. We can set our expectations on the results because they will not waver if we seek first the kingdom of heaven. It is as simple as that: believe in Him and have eternal life.

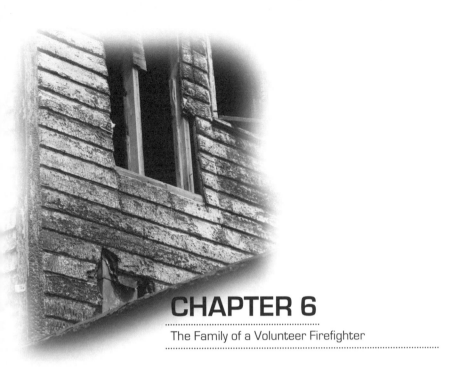

CHAPTER 6

The Family of a Volunteer Firefighter

My wife June is a music teacher in an elementary school. She has completed her administrative certification and is very bright. On top of that, she is beautiful. She said she married me for a rich future, but I was in college and my draft number for the army was very low. She saw into the future more than I did at that time. She has always been supportive of my many ventures: from the fire department to election to city council and my professional administrative work for public schools.

We were told that joining the fire department was a family decision. Every member of the family would be affected by the activities of Dad responding to calls. Dinners would be interrupted or the family would be left at church without a car. Sometimes the family got a joy ride when a call came over the pager as we were returning to the area from dinner or shopping.

Sometimes there were embarrassing moments, such as the times the fire whistle went off during church. My poor son Jeff, who was three or four years old, often got tongue-tied in the excitement and forgot the T's in his words, especially when yelling, "Dad has to go to the fire *uck." For some reason, his T's came out as F's. Buck claimed to have taught him the method.

The pager sat in its charger on the nightstand. When it went off at night, I would jump out of bed and quickly put on my sweat clothes. June would finally get the light on and open the door just as I grabbed my boots that were always at the door. Everything was like a well-oiled machine. The only problem occurred when my creative music teacher wife decided to change the bedroom around. The well-oiled machine usually got his oil changed by a newly positioned dresser.

One evening, our toddler son Jeff experienced some restlessness and fell asleep on the floor in the doorway of our bedroom. It was a good thing he was yelling his usual twisted fire truck words as the tone was sounding or who knows where the emergency would have been.

Sometimes family members were involved involuntarily. One night, Old Nick Schmidt had a problem after a midnight run. When we returned to the station and completed our cleanup detail, we usually went into the office to sign the roster indicating our position on the call: driver, responder, or standby, etc. We usually had a cup of good, hot, full-of-caffeine, black coffee to warm us up and "settle us down" before going back home to bed. We were always readjusting our clothes that we had put on in a hurry as we flew out the door from home.

That night, Nick was having trouble buttoning his shirt, and thought that he had misaligned the buttons with the holes. The problem was that the buttons were on the wrong side and he was wearing his wife's blouse. Can you imagine sitting in a fire hall with six or eight of your buddies looking at you in your wife's pink-and-blue blouse? When we told him a bra was caught in his belt on the back, he almost believed us. We only hoped that he'd gotten the right underwear on and we could not resist suggesting what kind of night he and his wife had been experiencing.

A classic event happened when my wife, the music teacher, made an appointment for a piano tuner to come to our house for the annual tune-up. It was a quiet Saturday afternoon in the summer. This was the first time that this particular man had been to our house to do the tuning. He was a small, frail, middle-aged man, and very much a perfectionist. He reminded me of a little scaredy-cat that would jump through the ceiling if a book dropped on the floor. I was working in the basement that warm day because it was cool down there. I could hear the piano tuner upstairs hitting the same keys over and over again. I did not have my fire department pager on me at the time, so when it went off in the bedroom, my wife, knowing I would not have heard the tone, moved quickly through the house past the piano tuner and yelled from the top of the basement stairs, "Fire!" I heard every key of the piano played at once and an anguished solo of, "Oh, my God" come from the hapless tuner. My wife spent the rest of the afternoon calming the poor guy down with cups of tea.

Our children were very much affected by my work as a volunteer firefighter. In the morning, the kids would get up and see my boots at the front door, perhaps with a bit of blood on them that hadn't gotten washed off the night before in the dark. They always asked, "Was the person drunk again?" Almost always the answer was yes, someone had been drinking and was trying to drive again.

It is interesting that later in her teens, my daughter Christy became a decoy for the local police department, checking stores that were selling alcohol to minors. My son, Jeff, became the president of his high school SADD chapter. I did not have to explain anything to them – the proof was on the boots. At Christmas one year, the kids thought that their Christmas stockings that always hung on our fireplace were too small in proportion to how good they had been all year, so they substituted Dad's fire boots. I couldn't resist filling them as full as I could.

A common error by new firefighters was to be called on the phone by the newbie's spouse at the fire hall. At the end of each run, we called the dispatcher on the radio to indicate that our station was back in service. The dispatcher returned our message with our time out and time in numbers. This was our signal that we were free to return home to our families. If a spouse happened to hear the call on the radio at home, she would sometimes call the firefighter by phone at the fire hall and ask him to pick up milk and bread, etc. on the way home. Of course, the assistant chief invariably answered the phone with something like, "Oh, he's not here. He never showed up. Must have stopped at his girlfriend's house."

As the poor victim of the call tried to get the phone, other responses and sounds filled the background such as a faux female voice saying something like, "Come back, Randy, don't go home, I want you!"

▼

I remember one time when Buck was responding to the fire hall from his home, which was on a side street. He was responding with full lights flashing and siren blaring. Another pickup was coming from the main street and would not yield right-of-way to Buck. A police car was nearby and witnessed the situation and pulled the unyielding pickup driver over. When the officer approached the pickup, he noticed a shopping cart with its contents of groceries in the back. The bad guy had just stolen an older woman's groceries in the parking lot of the food store – cart, groceries, purse, and all.

The report was just coming in to dispatch from the store where the incident had happened. The cop held up the guy long enough to hear the report on his radio. The guy ended up in jail for speeding, theft of over one hundred dollars, failing to yield to an emergency vehicle, and threatened assault. My buddy, Buck, usually had a very special salute for people who would not yield to a fireman responding to a call. He did tell the guy later, "Next time your house is on fire or your child is choking on a toy, I'll just sit here on this side street in my truck while some jerk like you makes me wait."

Buck just could not stand the inconsiderate people who did not yield to police and other emergency vehicles. One afternoon, we were responding to a terrible multiple-car crash on a busy interstate. It was rush hour and the right of way was completely blocked. I was driving and Buck was the radioman in the other seat. He was busy getting the details from dispatch as to the nature of the incident so we could direct the men in the back regarding what equipment we would need. I was left with no alternative as a driver but to drive on the grassy median to get around all the stopped traffic on this busy interstate.

The rarely-observed law of using the left expressway lane for passing only is on the books so that when emergency vehicles do show up, there is space for cars to pull over to the right so we have room to pass. There was simply nowhere for these people to move in their stopped cars to get out of our way. We were barreling our way down the dirt and grass of the median with lights on and siren squealing in a 1250 pumper fire truck just inches from the cars on our right. Suddenly, just a few yards ahead of us, a man opened wide the door of his luxury car and stepped out to get a better view of the situation ahead. Buck said, "Look at that stupid jerk opening a car door in front of us with all the noise we're making."

With a sick grin, Buck pulled the cord to our huge, dual chrome-plated air horns. The man acted so quickly, it was as if his car was equipped with a gigantic vacuum and the man was sucked back into the car and the door sealed up the opening in an instant. Buck said he was going to order a set of those horns for his pickup.

After Glow

A fire truck speeding to the scene of a family that needed our services was always a challenge because people did not always move out of the way and yield to the emergency vehicle. We used air horns, sirens, and flashing lights, but they often did not see or hear us coming. Can you imagine this person driving a car toward you in the other lane as well? If they could only put themselves in our situation or the situation of the terrified family who needs our services immediately! Time was always so critical to a successful call.

God sure knew what he was doing when he sent His Son to live the life of a human like us. John 1:14 reminds us that Christ became a human being and lived here on earth to feel love and forgiveness. Showing us that He clearly understands how we feel when terrified and when loved, He put himself in our shoes to prove that by following a life of forgiveness and mercy, we can have true happiness. God's Son is our emergency vehicle to heaven. If that concept is not clear to you, then you need to pull over and let the emergency vehicle of His love help you.

CHAPTER 7
Cat and Dog Stories

I do not have a particular attitude about cats. When I was growing up, we always had a cat or two and a dog. As my children were growing up, my daughter had a cat. For reasons that I do not recall, we never had my daughter's cat spayed. For the most part, the cat stayed in the house, so it did not seem to be a problem. In the winter, we usually enclosed an outside porch area at the back of our house. We used plastic sheeting to make a winter storage for our fireplace wood and patio furniture. A sliding patio door provided access to the firewood, but did not provide an exit to the outside.

During the winter, I would often allow the cat to go out into the porch to climb on the firewood. This would assure me that no mice had found places in the wood for the winter. It was during that special time when a cat is not spayed that an old tomcat began to frequent our home. The odor and the damage that this tom was causing to our deck and wood trim became more than we could tolerate. For six days,

I could not find the owner or a diversion for the old tom. His health looked poor and I was concerned for my family by the presence of the animal. In an effort to save our home and family from further damage, I had to destroy the tom. The firemen got word of the story and I started getting lots of harassment about eliminating the old tomcat.

Within a week of the incident, another cat was killed on the road in front of the fire hall. As the driver of the fire truck on a call, I had noticed the dead cat on the road as we pulled out of the station. I, of course, was blamed for running over the cat with the fire truck as we left the station. Everyone had seen that the cat was already dead and I drove around the site as I pulled the fire truck out of the station, but somebody was due on the harassment list and I guess my number was up.

A short time later, a house fire was reported just a few addresses down the street from my in-laws' home. I was on the tailboard on this incident, so I would be in the heat of this fire. We fought the fire for better than an hour and we did save the structure of the house. However, the contents were heavily smoke damaged and in disarray.

After the fire was out, we were doing our usual overhaul of the scene. Overhaul includes getting our equipment inventoried, securing the area for the owner, and looking for a possible cause of the fire. We also go through the debris with the owner to look for valuable papers, a safe, or other important items before we leave the site. As the chief was talking to the husband, the wife screamed loudly, "Oh, my poor Buffy!" We, of course, thought that the owners had forgotten to tell us that a child was missing or some other disaster had befallen, but the problem was that the family cat was missing.

The family had not been at home at the time of the fire. We were called by neighbors who saw smoke coming from the house and could not get the owners to answer the phone. Finally, after all the commotion had died down, the wife realized that the pet cat was probably locked inside with the fire. That was when my "good" friend, Lieutenant Barry Elinpunski yelled, "Davis! Do a search of the house and find the family cat." All the other firefighters started laughing at me, but immediately suppressed their delight in my assignment so as not to offend the owner. But they were having fun just the same as the cat hater (in their opinion) was looking for a presumably dead cat.

I approached the owner for information about the cat. Generally, when a crisis such as a fire occurs, a house pet will go to an area where it feels safe or where it sleeps. The lady told me that the cat usually hid under the bed in the daughter's room and sometimes in the closet when frightened. The house was still off limits except for fire personnel. Everything was black with a thick coating of soot. It was like a black-and-white photo except everything had a slightly altered appearance. For example, the living room chair looked like a chair, but the color and fabric was just black. You could not tell the difference between a rug and a towel on the blackened floor.

When I approached the daughter's bedroom, it appeared to be decorated with shelves and shelves of no less than five hundred stuffed animals. They were stacked on chairs, lying on beds, hanging from the ceiling, and attached to the door with hooks. There was very little room to walk. The soot made them all look the same except for the size of each precious little animal. How was I going to find a cat in this mess? With all of my gear still on, including air tanks, I began my search under the bed only to find more of the same. Even the closet was full of these creatures. I returned outside and asked the owner the approximate size of the cat and more specifically where it might go to hide or sleep.

After returning to search again to no avail, I went to the chief and said that it was impossible to find a cat among the other numerous cat-like objects in the room. He suggested that I take the owner into the house to help me locate the animal. When we were clear to take her into the house, I removed my tank, face shield, and Nomex fireproof headgear, but kept my helmet and other gear on. I braced her walk through the debris as we approached the bedroom. Just as we began to enter the bedroom, the lady let out a scream that curled up all our hose lines right up to the truck. She must have launched the chief straight up in the air because he was at my side in a matter of seconds. He translated the scream to the words, "My precious Buffy!"

At that moment, we were standing in the hallway at the door of the bedroom. Across from the doorway was the linen closet. There was reason to believe that the fire had started in the linen closet, so the first attack team had emptied the closet of all the towels, sheets and so forth onto the floor with no concern for tidiness. As a result, we were standing on heaps of wet, soot-covered laundry. That is, she was standing on heaps of dirty, soggy laundry. I, on the other hand, was standing on soot-covered dead cat. The lady sprinted from the scene across wet, soot-covered carpet, soaked drywall, and charred furniture.

I picked up the unfortunate feline by the legs and carried it to the door where Chief Vinny stood waiting to offer a bit of advice. He said this was not a hunting trip and that I should not carry the cat like a rabbit from the woods. He suggested I find a bag or box so I could present the cat to the lady in a covered situation. By the time we got back to the fire hall to join the other firefighters who hadn't gone on the run, the rumor had reached monstrous proportions. It was said that I had the cat slung over my shoulder by the back legs, proudly showing the lady what I had found.

At the annual fireman's dinner, I was presented with everything from a black cat coffee mug to various books on what to do with dead cats. The books offered over two hundred ways to creatively use dead cats. The joke around the fire hall was that the next time we got a call for a cat stuck up in a tree I would be sent with my pickup and hunting equipment. There would be no need for ladders.

▼

When I was a young child, my mom would read to me about the friendly policemen and firefighters. The book would show a police officer directing traffic and the firefighters would be washing their truck and petting a Dalmatian dog. The familiar white dog with the black spots has been known as the firefighter's friend. I am not sure of the origin of this belief, but the tradition continues.

We were planning an upcoming parade with our dress uniforms and polished trucks. I suggested to the guys that it might be a great idea to have a Dalmatian with us on the truck during the parade. One of the men gave me the name of a family who might let us use their Dalmatian for the event. I called the family and they agreed to allow the dog to be used, but insisted that the owner had to be near the dog at all times. I thought the owner was trying to get a free ride on a fire truck in a parade in front of his friends. I found out otherwise.

He did happen to mention that the dog was a little touchy. On the day of the parade, the dog arrived just in time, as the truck needed to leave the hall for our position in the parade. I asked Chief Vinny to help me lift the dog up to the top of the truck with me. This area is covered with a canvas that protects the hose bed of the truck. As we lifted the dog over our heads, the dog snapped and bit my shoulder, tearing my uniform and barely missing my ear. The owner said, "I told you the dog was a little touchy."

On the next attempt, the owner and I managed to lift the dog onto the hose bed successfully. The dog continued to growl horribly and Chief Vinny was sharing my dilemma with the rest of the department as fast as he could. The owner stayed on the tailboard of the truck in the dog's view as I rode on the canvas next or fairly near the dog. I smiled and waved to the kids and families that were taking pictures of the fire dog. All the while, the dog clenched her teeth and lifted her lip in a sadistic scowl. The guttural sounds continued until the owner took her home, for which I was grateful.

I was president of our fire association that year, so I had the pleasure of sending the thank you note to the family for sharing their family pet with the community. Another great idea bit the dust.

I have since read an e-mail about a group of school children that were asked the question of why the firefighters used Dalmatian dogs. Their response was so that the firefighters can quickly find the fire hydrants.

After Glow

To keep a pet healthy, it is important to keep food and water available for it daily. Exercise is also necessary for a happy, content pet. Spending time with your pet keeps it loyal to you and it gets excited when you return home.

John 6:35 tells us that God is the bread of life and that those that believe in Him will never go hungry and never thirst. Other instructions include daily study and exercise of His Word. I think if we do these things, we will be excited when God brings us home.

CHAPTER 8

The Subdivision Picnic

As a community service, the fire department often raises money for charity. We hold an open house for fire safety week in October, teach CPR, supply smoke alarms to senior citizens, and provide many other benefits for our neighborhoods.

One August afternoon we were asked to bring a fire truck to a subdivision picnic. One area of our town had a large enough subdivision that the developers provided land for an elementary school and a small community park. We were often asked to bring a fire truck to the park for the kids to see and we let them blow the siren and pull the cords for the air horns. We topped off the experience by setting up a gentle spray from a fire hose for the kids to operate. Their friends ran or rode their bikes through the spray, which, on a hot day, was refreshing. Sometimes we hooked up to a hydrant to make a full-blown shower.

After a certain hot afternoon of this type of fun, some of the adults approached our crew of four. They offered to give us some cold beer with a few extras to take back to the fire hall. We, of course, had to refuse, but did stay for a hot dog and a cold pop. It was just as I was getting the mustard on my hot dog that we got a call for a medical emergency at a car accident some three miles away. We had a truck ready for service already manned with four firemen. We called dispatch on the truck radio and told them we would take the call. The picnic group thought we were cool exiting the park with lights and siren just like on TV.

When we arrived at the scene of the accident, I stopped the fire truck and we began to assess the situation. We approached the side compartments of our truck to get the first aid equipment and the Jaws of Life ready for use. Just as we opened the compartments, we found that they were packed full of beer from our grateful picnic folks. The cans fell everywhere: some rolling on the road under cars and others bursting open, spraying generously as they hit the hard pavement. It seemed that our picnic friends wanted to thank us for volunteering our day for their party. They had apparently hoped that their surprise would be discovered at the fire hall after inspection when we put the truck back in service.

The people injured in the accident were shocked at the sight and exhibited all kinds of nervous gestures as we began to administer first aid. Some of the injured who were able to communicate with some degree of understanding asked many questions such as, "Where in the world did you come from?" "What else do you carry in that truck?" "You must have a lot of time on your hands."

I could just imagine what the chief would say if he happened to select this run to check out our work or if he got a letter sometime later from the people in the accident. The bigger dilemma was what were the police, who were assisting and writing reports, supposed to do? As a school administrator, I have heard a lot of excuses for bad choices by expert high school delinquents. This gave me the advantage over the others in creating a likely story to put everyone at ease. When the lady in the accident asked me where in the world we came from, I told her that we were just returning from another "incident." The beer cans and all of this stuff were cleaned up from the other "incident." Seeing how both drivers from this accident had been drinking, they understood and the rest of the group who knew me started coughing from what I assume was trouble swallowing the story. My fireman friends indicated that they were glad that they had boots on.

After Glow

Just like the unwanted gift from the people of the subdivision, we occasionally receive gifts from people that are just the opposite of our desires and needs. This usually reflects on the fact that the giver does not really know us very well or that not much thought was given to the relationship of the gift to our interests. When we take the time to truly appreciate others, then our gifts will celebrate our appreciation of that person in our family or as a friend.

Our gifts to our Heavenly Father will also reflect on how well we know Him. As immature Christians, we simply go to church and put a small gift in the offering plate. As we mature in our faith, our gifts become tithes and offerings resulting in a percentage of our income. We give our gifts of time and talents to Him through helping others and sometimes the church is the avenue toward that end.

Giving our time and talents to His glory are gifts, but if the time and talents are for our own edification, then the gift is the opposite of God's desires and needs. We are instructed to be cheerful givers in 2 Corinthians 9:7-9. We are not to be forced to give, but free to give as we choose. It is the cheerful giver whom God prizes.

CHAPTER 9

Chap and the Bad Guy

During tornado warnings and watches, our fire stations were always put on standby status. That meant we were required to respond to the station and take the trucks to each of the four corners of the community and act as spotters for threatening clouds. On one of these standbys, I was the driver of one of the fire trucks parked in a shopping center parking area standing watch. Buck was also in the cab with me as we reported our visual findings to the dispatch.

After having sat for about a half hour, Chap, one of the other volunteer firemen, raced up in the chief's car alongside the truck. His eyes were wide with alarm as he jumped up onto the running board of my truck. The window was rolled down and we were face to face as he yelled for me to take the chief's car back to the corner near the station immediately as there was an emergency. He said that my wife had a thief cornered in some bushes by the river and the police were on the way.

I smiled inwardly. There was no way I was going to fall for that whopper of a story. It had been just two weeks before that I had pulled a fast one on my buddy Chap.

Chap's last name was Kukuk, pronounced like a cuckoo clock. Chap and his wife were substituting in our bowling league that week and I was able to get to the couple who were going to be their bowling partners before Chap arrived. I told this nice couple that their substitutes that night were friends of mine and they loved pulling tricks on people. I told them that, as a joke, he would arrive and introduce himself as Chap Kukuk (cuckoo) and always liked to see how people reacted to that funny name. When Chap finally arrived, the couple did as I expected, and Chap had to pull out his driver's license before they would put his name on the bowling sheet. In short, I was due for a few paybacks.

The corner I was stationed at was two blocks from my house and my lovely wife, while courageous, is not the sort who would corner a thief in some bushes. Buck's belly laugh added to my certainty that this was a payback trick. Buck's wife and my wife were good friends, and he knew as well as I did that this was an impossible story.

However, Chap was so frustrated that I would not take him seriously that he opened the truck door and physically hauled me out of the vehicle. Chap is a huge man and when he wanted something moved, it usually moved by itself just because of the expression on his face. He said, "Get your butt to town, your wife needs you." I finally relented, as I saw the opportunity to drive the chief's car and be a big shot in town. By this time, I think Buck was sorry the joke was on me and not on him.

I responded to the street corner in the chief's car with lights and siren. After all, it was my wife who was in trouble and needed my help. When I arrived at the corner, sure enough, there was my wife in front of a crowd of people pointing to the bushes as the police, with weapons drawn, flushed out a thief.

The episode had started when a local teenager wandered casually into our open garage area and helped himself to a couple eight packs of empty pop bottles. He would turn them in for the deposit to help offset the price of cigarettes. The storeowner later said that the kid probably would have stolen the cigarettes and then requested the money for the deposit on the bottles. He had obviously experienced problems with this particular miscreant before.

The kid had been casually walking across our lawn with the bottles when my wife yelled to him. She told him that he couldn't just take those bottles, that he was stealing. She was not familiar with this young man in our neighborhood, and as she yelled, he simply kept walking as if he knew she would do nothing about the situation. He picked up the pace a bit when my barefooted wife took off, chasing him for two blocks. She yelled to our neighbors as she ran by their houses to call the police. She continued to chase the kid to the end of the road, where he hid under the bridge at the river. This was a big deal in our little town, we didn't get too much excitement in those days. From the bridge, the kid ran out to the bushes, where he thought he could hide while they were looking for him under the bridge. To his misfortune, my wife was an elementary music teacher, and those eyes she had in the back of her head saw him make the move.

As it turned out, the guy had already missed a court date for several other pilfering and shoplifting charges. He was arrested on the spot and jailed. I had to apologize to Chap for not believing his story.

Chap, being a big man, had large cheeks and his words were sometimes misunderstood in an emergency. I remember a time when we arrived on the scene of a leg injury where a young man had fallen out of a tree. When a person had seriously injured a leg, it was standard procedure to take a pedal pulse. That is, we took a person's pulse at the top of the foot to see if circulation had been interrupted. Chap, in his excited voice, explained to the young man that he was going to take his pedal pulse and it sounded like he said his penile pulse. Chap was big and the young man was small but there was a general show of concern on the young man's face. He asked what his penis had to do with the injury, and Chap could not believe his ears. Chap said, "It has nothing to do with your private thing. Why do you think I would want to touch that anyway?" Chap looked at me with that sick, Hoss Cartwright look on his face as if to say, "How did I get into this one?" I simply smiled and said, "Chap, you are so darn thorough, everything has become a habit for you, but I think we can move along now as I have found a strong *pedal* pulse.

After Glow

Words, especially in the English language, often have more than one meaning. A slight change in the makeup of a word can put you in a situation like that of our buddy Chap. But because Chap was with a friend, the meaning and pronunciation of his garbled words made sense to someone who knew him personally.

Studying God's Word with other Christians gives us a clearer understanding of His plan for us. Attending classes, formal and informal discussions, and sermons are all opportunities for us to become better students of the Scriptures. As we become more fluent with His Word, we begin to see our gifts and may find ourselves leading classes or discussions to provide others with a better understanding of His plan. Getting to know God personally will help eliminate misunderstood words and messages.

CHAPTER 10

On Pins and Needles

After what seemed like a long period of time with no calls or needs for the fire department, we finally received a very unusual call. Years ago, the citizens band (CB) radio was popular. Everyone had a CB in his car or truck. Our police department received a call while monitoring channel nineteen. The old familiar, "Breaker one nine for a Smokey [state police] report," came across the air sharp and clear.

Then the usual response was, "Come back on that Smokey report."

The caller said, "This is the PeeWee, and I don't know where there is a Smokey, but we need one northbound on M-42."

Our local dispatcher replied, "We are the Meadowbrook Police Department. We are monitoring channel nineteen. Is there a problem?"

"Yes," came the reply. "This is the PeeWee, and I am going northbound on M-42. I am following a garbage truck that has smoke rolling out the back and I think it is going to explode. The paint on the side of the truck is peeling off and smoking as well."

In many communities, the police and fire departments do not often get along very well, but in Meadowbrook, we appreciated the cooperation of the two departments, especially on cold nights when some of our volunteer firemen opted to stay in a warm bed rather than respond to a call.

On this night, the police were dispatched to the trash truck and we were called to put the fire out as soon as the police found the location. Some minutes later, the police officer on the scene confirmed that there was an extremely hot fire in the back of a garbage truck and he asked for the fire department to step it up.

The fire had been smoldering for quite a while during the slow process of frequent stops. When the truck reached the open highway at speeds of about forty-five miles per hour, the fire developed an excellent draft. The driver was ending his day and was giving it the gas as he headed toward the landfill and therefore was unaware of the fire. The trash truck was an automatic dumpster truck that serviced commercial businesses. So it didn't help that the driver got out of the truck only when he had to open or close gates that were used to screen the dumpsters at various business sites.

After assessing the situation, Vinny, our assistant chief, ordered the driver to dump his load on the side of the highway so we could hose down the fire. The intense heat from the truck itself did not allow us to get anywhere near it. The mud flaps were melting off and the paint was burned away.

The heat intensified the sickening gob of goo, trash, and horrible odors. As one of my buddies said, it was "hot, boiling garbage available fresh on the side of the road."

The garbage had been compacted so tightly that when it was released, the huge truck left a mound some fifteen feet high. We had to call for another truck in order to have enough water to extinguish the smolder. We used long pike poles and shovels to roll and stir the stuff, getting water to the core where the fire seemed to have started. There was hair from beauty salons and barbershops, dead bait from the bait shop, and dead plants from the garden shop. We had our protective clothing on and our self-contained breathing tanks and masks. We climbed the pile and continued to spread the material.

Poor old Ed Hapman, one of our firefighters, was on the top of this mess when he lost his balance and fell first to his knees and then "mask to the trash fall." When he regained his balance and stood up, he complained of a prickling at his knees. As the rest of us examined Ed, we saw what was easily a four-letter-word problem. Ed had several needles, such as doctors use to give shots, sticking out of his knee and leg. We got him off the pile and rushed the needles and Ed in his trash-soaked gear off to the hospital. We asked the driver for a list of his stops in an effort to identify the source of the needles. He indicated that there were no doctor offices or clinics on his route. He couldn't remember all of the stops, as this was a new route for him. A call to the trash company provided us with a series of mechanical answering machine choices. Even after selecting a "press one," the machine said that it was after hours and that they would return our call the next day during regular business hours.

On Pins and Needles

At the hospital, they had to assume that the needles had in them what the code indicated in small print on the casings. Our buddy Ed had been inoculated for fleas. One of the stops on the trash route had indeed included a veterinary clinic for small animals. Actually, the flea shots were exactly what we thought Ed needed. His truck had an odor worse than his old basset hound. We were just glad to know that Ed would no longer be a threat to us with fleas. In fact, several months later we were fishing in Canada and noticed that the black flies and mosquitoes stayed away from Ed. We determined that the shots had long-lasting results for fleas and flies and we considered getting our own shots before the next fishing trip.

After Glow

Our protective clothing for the fire service allowed us to get a little bit closer to danger in order to be swift and efficient in our effort to remedy the emergency. As a result, we were able to put out what could have been a very dangerous fire.

There is an old hymn that suggests that we put on the gospel armor. It goes on to say that each piece should be put on with prayer. Ephesians 6:11-18 tells exactly what to put on and how it will protect us from the dangers of the world.

This world hits us with lots of garbage and if we don't prepare ourselves with His protective Word, then we may find ourselves being needled to death by the garbage that man has created by following evil desires.

CHAPTER 11

Saved From Hell

One of the most unusual blazes I have ever fought was that of a swamp fire. At the north end of our community was a large lowland area. It was very dry from several years of less-than-normal rainfall. The rich, black, dry swamp bed made ideal conditions for this unique kind of fire.

The source of the fire was unknown and all we could see was smoke. The fire was underground. It was a late August fire that burned for nearly two weeks. The roots of huge trees completely burned through, undermining their foundations and allowing them to crash to the ground with thunderous shakes of the earth. Even late at night, the area was flooded with emergency lights in the haze of the smoke and intense heat. The trees with their roots burned away fell in front of us and behind us at the most inopportune moments. We attempted to flood the area with water, especially where the smoke was the most intense.

The work continued in eight-hour shifts. Each day we asked our regular employers for time off to stay with the fire department to neutralize this community hazard. The nearby churches had food available around the clock for the firefighters. The local ambulance was parked nearby, news reporters were everywhere, and we just could not get the fire extinguished. It mysteriously kept creeping out of control no matter how hard we worked to flood the area with water.

Later, we moved in heavy equipment to turn the swamp upside down to get at the hot ash that seemed to be feeding the never-ending smoke and heat. The situation was extremely dangerous as the large trees continued to fall without warning, sometimes within a few feet of the emergency team. The wear and tear on men and equipment was so much that we began to wonder if letting it burn might be a better option.

Finally, the Department of Natural Resources got involved with their vast amount of resources and knowledge. We dug a wide perimeter ditch deep into the ground, then flooded the trench, so that when the fire reached that point, it would burn itself out. In one higher area, we back-burned a wide strip so that when the fire reached that area, there would be nothing left to burn and the fire would die out. We were fighting fire with fire as they say.

It was a long battle, taking every last ounce of energy we could muster day after day. One of the guys said that walking on that hot ground, feeling the heat, and breathing the smoke everywhere, was like walking in hell. I had not thought about comparing the situation we were in to that of hell, but it did make me take another look at just how I might be living my life. This was not how I hoped to spend eternity.

I had recently been approached by some church members to take on a leadership position and I had refused them almost without giving it any thought at all. Now I began to think that God was working in one of those mysterious ways. The leadership job at the church would not take nearly as much time as I was spending here in hell. As I thought again about eternity, a light came on in my mind: hell or heaven. I would look to see if the position was filled at the church, and maybe even take in a potluck or two in the process. Some of that home-cooked fried chicken and those homemade rolls and pies in the church basement sure looked better than what I knew hell looked like, because I had been there.

▼

Later in my career with the department, Reverend Cypress, who had been the department chaplain, resigned. He said it was time for the younger guys to take his position and that his availability was getting more limited. Now that I am a little older and off the department, there are a few things I have found that have limited my availability to respond as well. However I would have spelled availability with a "C" and said "capability." It hurts to push doors down, pull hose lines, climb ladders, and do it all at breakneck speed in the middle of the night half dressed under your turnout gear.

When Rev. Cypress made his announcement, the department chief approached me about being the new department chaplain. He had heard that I had "seen the light" after the swamp fire and was a church elder. I had also been fairly articulate in my remarks at T.H. Florson's funeral. I told the chief that I would have to think about it first and that I would let him know in a week or so.

That week, we had a huge field fire that spread toward some thick woods and visions of the swamp fire returned to my memory. I found the chief later that day and said, sure, I would be glad to be the department chaplain. He seemed surprised about my uncertainty a few days before and my enthusiasm later. He said, "Did you see another light?"

I said, "I sure did, and it keeps blinking every so often."

The chief said he would like to talk to me about it sometime as he had never seen any lights like that before. He was wondering why I was the one getting all these light messages when his message machine light never seemed to flash. I told the chief that I knew the road to heaven and the road to hell and that I just follow the lights. But the lights that are kind of a fiery red, I avoid.

As the new chaplain, I made hospital calls to firefighters and their families. I spoke at the funerals and in general, counseled members in a host of problems. I was surprised at the amount of work that the job required and how much of it was never seen by the general membership of the department. It became harder to do that part of the job than the actual firefighting.

When I was finally ready to hang up my turnout gear and turn it over to the 'younger" guys and now gals, I was asked to consider continuing as the chaplain. This relieved me of getting up in the middle of the night, but on really big fires, I was able to lend an extra hand and not take up a position on the roster.

We unfortunately lost a fireman a few years later, and it took everything from me to work through the family of the firefighter and the guys at the stations. What made it all the more difficult was the fact that both the fallen firefighter and his wife (who was pregnant with their first child) were former students of mine and I knew them very well. The chaplain's position turned out to be a tough job that I had taken on with little appreciation for what needed to be done.

It all turned around when I found myself in the hospital. Just before Christmas, I was taking a few students to my hunting camp in the Upper Peninsula of Michigan. On the trip north I had a terrible stomachache. I was usually able to get rid of such discomfort in short order, so I continued the trip. That night, I found myself on the edge of a stream near the camp trying to drink water but continuing to vomit. When it did not go away by morning, I thought I might be in trouble. I wanted to be near familiar doctors and hospitals, so I asked the students to drive my truck back home with me wrapped in a blanket. They even had to fix a flat tire on the way. When we arrived home, I had a quick checkup and was in surgery that night for a ruptured appendix. It was close, but I survived after nearly a week in the hospital.

My buddies back at the fire department were concerned that there was no one designated to make sure that my family was going to be OK, especially during the holidays. They wanted to visit and I told my wife I did not want visitors as the stitches hurt and my chest was congested. The last thing I wanted was the harassment of the guys even when I knew it was well-meaning. Of course, they did not listen and showed up anyway with a huge spray of flowers wrapped in green florist's paper. It was the biggest bundle I had ever seen even though I could not see the actual flowers. They had me laughing and coughing the minute they walked into the room. The nurse came in and said it was good that I was coughing and getting the congestion worked out of my system.

As the nurse was leaving she remarked, "What is that awful smell?" I was sure it was Buck, as he had no scruples as to where he passed wind, and in fact was proud that he was so effective at the most opportune times. But it was not Buck this time. The nurse said she thought it was coming from the flowers.

Truth be told, I was really surprised that the guys would spend money on flowers. As guys, we thought that buying cut flowers was a waste of money, as they would just die anyway. We were so cheap that back at the station, we didn't buy cream or sugar for coffee. Everybody learned to drink rich, black coffee. Of course, we always asked if people wanted cream and sugar but they never got any. So why would these cheap guys buy me flowers? The truth was about to be known.

On the way to the hospital, the guys had passed a graveyard. They found a new grave and took the gigantic casket spray of flowers to bring to me. The fact is, the blooms were pretty old and the lovely odor made that fact very clear. I am sure my recovery was enhanced by several days by a bunch of guys taking the time to check on an old buddy. Even my family changed its long tradition of Christmas at Grandpa and Grandma's house and had Christmas at my house that year as I recovered from surgery.

After Glow

We never know when in our daily lives we might be the one that will save a person from hell. Some people have influenced me and I was never given the opportunity to learn their names.

It is always important to be mindful of the needs of others. It is also important to ask for help when we find ourselves with needs and questions. Too often, people think that a Christian who has problems has a weak faith. Sometimes the problem, when resolved, is the nucleus for your opportunity to help others with a similar problem in the future.

In the words of Isaiah 6:8, the Lord asks, "Whom shall I send?" It may be you whom He needs to help save a person from destruction. The Lord truly works in mysterious ways, but when we follow His lead, the journey is fun and memorable.

CHAPTER 12

Santa is Smoked Out

My son, Jeff, along with many other of the firemen's sons, was active in Cub Scouts. While in elementary school, he attended his pack meetings once a week, and in fact became a heavily decorated little Cub Scout. His uniform still hangs on the wall in our recreation room. At the end of the year, there was an annual cookie baking competition. Each Cub Scout, along with his father, was to bake some cookies. Then at the Christmas party, the Cub Master and a couple of community people would judge the cookie entries for first, second, and third place.

Jeff and I selected his mom's big gingerbread man cookie cutter. We baked up some beautiful cookies with some technical advice from Mom. After they were cooled, we decorated the little cookie men to look like little Cub Scouts, complete with official colors and hats. They were perfect. In fact, they were so perfect that they were disqualified because the judges thought that we bought them at a bakery. Jeff was really disappointed and even using my influence as a city councilman (politician) did not get us anywhere.

It was a double letdown for Jeff as he had just been disqualified in the final races of the model car pinewood derby. He was told late in the derby competition that he could not use a previous year's entry, which had won him district honors the past year. He had made only slight modifications in hopes of winning a place at the state level. We had no idea that a car could not be reused.

So even though Jeff was progressing well in the ranks as a scout, his special project entries were a big disappointment. And the end-of-year Christmas cookie competition was the final blow. As soon as I had Jeff accepting his second undeserved disqualification in a row, my fire pager went off and I had to run to the fire hall to answer the call. It turned out to be a false alarm and I was heading back to the Cub Scout meeting, which was going to wrap up with an appearance of Santa Claus.

There was only one problem. Santa had not shown up. The jolly old gentleman that we all used for Santa at our community functions was very late. Usually, a big box of cigars was all that was required to convince him to play his role and arrive on time. It appeared that someone had offered him a better deal at the local bar and Santa was not coming. The Cub Scout leaders saw me in the parking lot as I was returning from the false alarm. They cornered me and said that it was imperative that I be Santa this year. They tried to persuade me by saying the boys would never guess it was me because they thought I was off fighting a fire or some other emergency. I told them that there was no way I could do this after the disappointment my son had received from these folks. After receiving the same lecture I gave to Jeff about disappointment, I was Santa in about fifteen minutes. So, ho ho ho, the line started to form for the opportunity to sit on Santa's lap. I began listening to the long list of Christmas wishes from boys who claimed absolute innocence of any wrongdoing during the past year. I was glad the adults of this Cub Scout group didn't suggest the same innocence.

As it turned out, this was working in my favor. You see, our son Jeff would not share his wish list with anyone. He figured that if he shared the list only with Santa, he could prove whether or not there was a Santa. So in my new role as Santa I would get to see the list and Jeff would not be the wiser. As the line worked its way down, Jeff was patiently getting closer to the front of the line. When his turn came, he climbed up on my lap and I said the usual "ho ho ho" with real gusto. Jeff looked into my eyes and whispered, "Dad!" He was humiliated. His pinewood derby car had been disqualified, his cookies had been disqualified, and he disqualified Santa by smoking out his identity, at least quietly to himself. He walked away without his Santa candy cane and mumbled something about quitting the Cub Scouts and filing a claim for abused and neglected kids. He never joined the Boy Scouts, but he sure tore up the court in floor hockey setting records at the local Boys' Club.

After Glow

When we disappoint others or others disappoint us, it is important to resolve the issue as soon as possible. Compassion, forgiveness, and honesty are essential to end the disappointment. The bond of a family member or a friend is often stronger after an understanding has been reached. Usually, misinformation or lack of information is often at the core of the disappointment.

Luke 6:41-42 makes no excuses for us and clearly tells us to clean up our own acts before attempting to help others with their problems. How can you see clearly to the heart of another's problem if you have not cleaned up your own mess? It is hard to witness to others when our own conflicts or disappointments are not resolved.

CHAPTER 13

Getting Burned On My Fortieth

Turning forty years old in our little community was big news, especially if you were even remotely related to someone on the fire department. While I was in my thirties, I had great fun pulling pranks on unsuspecting people about to see the top of the hill. Of course, now, turning forty was a long time ago for me and it just does not seem that old anymore. Someone once told me that old is twenty years older than you are.

Buck and I had a good buddy, Tim Farmer, who turned forty on Memorial Day and we took advantage of the situation by putting a large sign on the side of the fire truck in the Memorial Day parade. It simply announced that Tim was thirty-nine yesterday but not today. If I recall correctly, we even got the mayor to pray for the passing of his youth as he spoke about the history of the area's service people.

Buck's wife was the next one to make the mark of forty and I put Burma Shave-type signs in her front yard suggesting that drivers honk their horns as they passed by the house to wish her a happy birthday. There was construction going on at the end of her street. The 6:00 AM cement trucks had a ball that morning with their air horns.

A friend at work who was a career bachelor was my next victim. I put an ad in the local paper which said, "Forty-year-old bachelor needs woman who cleans and cooks fish, and owns her own boat." The ad suggested that they send a picture of the boat and I included his address and phone number. Our local school bus drivers (all women) joined the fun and began calling him at all hours. He finally installed the answering machine that he'd sworn he would never succumb to purchasing.

The best one, however, was when my old buddy Buck hit forty years old. I gave a lot of thought to what I could possibly do to top all the other pranks that he and I usually engineered. With only about two weeks left before the big day, I was still at a loss for a creative solution. It all changed on my way home from work one tired evening. There on the side of the road was a good old-fashioned dunk tank, with a sign on it that said "For Rent." Wow, the Lord does work in wonderful ways. Buck said later that it was the devil, not the Lord at work that day.

I immediately left a check for a deposit and reserved the tank for a fortieth birthday party. I also bought two big rolls of tickets from the supply store and sold them all over the community for a nickel each. I wanted to sell them cheaply to get lots of people out to the dunking. I had to arrange for the tank to be set up in the fire hall because the October winds would have turned the dunk tank water into ice if left outside. We decided to have Buck's sons take him to the fire hall after dinner. When he saw all the streamers wishing him a happy birthday and the tank, all he could say was, "That water better be warm." I sure sold a lot of tickets and people sure wanted to get their nickel's worth. Old Buck looked like a tea bag dipping in and out of the water.

I remember the day I volunteered to sit in a dunk tank for a session for the school. The kids picked several community people whom they thought would draw a crowd to raise money for a school project. I thought I would put my all into the show so I wore an old suit and tie for the occasion. I stayed dry for a long time due to poor aim by the participants, but they finally found a baseball pitcher and just fed him their tickets. The problem was that I was wearing a wool necktie and as it got wet it began to shrink and slowly choke me. Everyone was laughing and having a great time as I began to panic in an effort to get the tie cut off. I think I saw Buck in the background, but it was hard to tell for sure who the guy was in the fetal position on the ground laughing.

I was probably the last to turn forty years old for some time. After that day, all the pranks seemed to lose their potency. Here I was, about to turn forty and nobody seemed to have a clue. Everybody around me stayed very quiet. In fact, as the day got closer I began to think that I was going to skate through this birthday without a scratch. Then I noticed that people began to avoid me and not even say hello. They started to call me Mr. Davis instead of the familiar Mike. My feeling of slyness at fooling everybody changed to shyness at fooling nobody. I began to take every precaution I could think of to watch my truck and my office.

At exactly the stroke of midnight on my fortieth birthday, a crowd gathered outside our bedroom window and began singing "Happy

Birthday." I slowly opened the curtain to see what was causing all the noise. I was in my underwear, safe in the dark background, looking out at the crowd when my wife flipped on the ceiling bedroom light that had three 100-watt bulbs. It was show time.

The folks were great sports and they brought cake and ice cream for a midnight snack with friends. It was a weeknight and we all had to go to work the next day. I felt fortunate to have friends who would sacrifice a good night's sleep for a guy who had been kind of rough with them on their fortieths.

The next day, my office staff had my office upside down, full of balloons and a box about three feet square sitting on my desk. It was from my bachelor friend who'd gotten the school bus drivers so excited. The box contained some rather old horse manure. The gnats, flies, and odor were released rather pungently when I opened the box. It had been on my desk for nearly twelve hours.

The next evening, it was drill night at the fire department and I enjoyed my favorite lemon pie from the guys who affectionately fed it to me in the face. The next day it was quiet and I decided that, all in all, I'd gotten off pretty easily, so I let my guard down, assuming everything to do with my being forty was past. I was wrong!

On Friday night, our friends, the Dukes, from out of town, were staying overnight at our house. Debbie Duke was from the area and we were going to have dinner with a few friends whom she had not seen for some time. I had cleaned the car and parked it at the end of the driveway so that we would not be blocked in when we were ready to leave for the restaurant. Across the street from our house was a deep ravine that was heavily wooded with trees and thick cover. I went out to the car to put my jacket in the trunk. Suddenly, from the woods across the street came these men in camouflage suits and women's nylon stockings on their heads and faces. They tackled me while a plumbing van pulled up next to our driveway. The men put a pillowcase over my head and duct-taped my hands and feet. I was thrown into the van and we sped off. In a strange, alien voice, the driver said that if I would just cooperate I would not get hurt.

I was on the local city council at the time. The previous Monday night, I had voted against a development by a landscape company. My speech had convinced the majority to follow my lead to cancel the project. The reason I objected was that I had learned that the company stored large hills of manure and that you would be able to smell it in a nearby neighborhood: namely, mine. I began to wonder what kind of power brokers I had angered.

I struggled against the people holding me, trying to memorize each turn in an effort to identify where we were going. It seemed to me that we were going nowhere and staying in the general area. In my struggle, I saw a watch and identified one pair of boots from one of the men. Trying to remember as much as I could, I realized that I had seen too much TV with this same scenario.

After about twenty or thirty minutes (it seemed like an hour) of driving around, we stopped and I was carried out of the van and into a building. It smelled like fresh laundry in a clean house and I was heading for the basement headfirst. I hoped that they had a good grip on me. It was dark and seemed very warm as I was laid on what felt like an ordinary table.

I was unwrapped to a crowd that began yelling, "Surprise!" and "Happy birthday!" My old buddy, Buck, had hired several kids from the local football team and his sons to help pull the project off so he could drive the van himself. The kids said that it was hard to be rough with me because they did not want to hurt me, yet they didn't want to allow me to break out of the van. There were times when I thought I might be stronger than my assailants and I considered breaking away if the episode had gone on longer. Buck said that we were fifteen minutes early bringing me to the party because he was afraid of what might happen at a stop sign and that the prank had gone on long enough. It was all in good fun, but I think I jumped from forty years old to fifty in the space of one evening while riding in that van. I know it was several more days before I felt it was safe to let my guard down once again.

I am still working on some future ideas for my aging friends. My dear sister, Patti, will turn fifty this year and I am considering sending her a new fire extinguisher to help blow out her candles. Her husband, Rich, a retired New York City firefighter, would appreciate the thought, I am sure. They live a long way away so I should be safe until reunion time.

After Glow

Someone once said that getting older is better than the alternative. The graying hair or disappearing hair is not an excuse to sit back and say our work for the Lord is done. On the contrary, older people have the wisdom of experience and it must be shared with younger people. If we don't do this, then the mistakes of our past will continue to be repeated. We have a responsibility to share our discoveries in our faith so that our children will understand God's love.

Proverbs 16:31 tells us that white hair is a crown of glory and is seen most among the godly. White hair is the light for our children to follow as they explore the adventures of the Scriptures.

CHAPTER 14

Homecoming

The high school homecoming football game is always a special time in a small town. In Meadowbrook, the parade was usually in early October. Our parade included floats from various organizations and classes from the school such as the seniors, the athletic boosters, the local SADD group, etc. These floats featured students throwing candy to the crowd. The convertibles carrying the homecoming queen candidates and the court were next in line. Fire trucks, police cars, and local politicians throwing out prizes and candy made up the nearly hour-long parade.

The marching band always led the parade just behind a police car that cleared traffic. My daughter, Christy, was a baton twirler in her first years of high school and later became the drum major for the band. It was in those early years that Christy decided she wanted to twirl fire batons during homecoming halftime. There was much discussion about the dangers of the idea and who would buy the

specially manufactured batons. Christy convinced the school and I
had to convince her mother that she should be given the privilege of at
least practicing.

After a lot of practice, it was decided that she could perform
during halftime with the band only if her dad, the fireman, would
remain on the field during the performance with a bucket of water in
the event a baton went out of control. There was concern that the long
hair on the twirler might catch fire. The bucket of water would be used
to pour over the lovely twirler if such an accident were to occur. Can
you imagine a father pouring a bucket of water on his sixteen-year-
old daughter in front of a grandstand of our friends and neighbors?
Her body language made it very clear that she had better be in grave
danger before I even thought about pouring that bucket of water on
her in public. As tempted as I was, especially with the encouragement
of my fellow firefighters in the stands, the bucket remained full and I
am enjoying grandchildren to this day.

▼

One year, while returning the fire truck from the parade to the fire
hall, we received a call for medical assistance at a Laundromat. The
dispatcher said that we would find a woman with her hand trapped
in a washing machine. When we arrived, we found the woman, but
her problems were far worse than they initially appeared. She had an
infant in a car seat with her in the laundry facility. She was new to the
area and the washing machine had not caught up with the family in the
move. Her clothes were done and she had decided to take the baby to

the car and strap her in the seat belt in the car seat. Then she moved the car to the front door from the parking lot. She parked the car in the fire lane, got out and closed and locked the door with the engine running and her purse (with the extra key) and the baby locked inside.

The Laundromat management called the police to open the car door as the frantic mother tried to get the one last sock that had lodged in a small crevice of the washing machine. That was when her hand got trapped, as if in a Chinese handcuff, in the washing machine. Management then called our fire rescue unit to help out as well. The police got the door open and we dismantled the washing machine to get the mother free.

Just as this situation seemed to get worse and worse for the lady, the solutions got better and better as well. You see, this mother had a coupon from the local Welcome Wagon for a "buy one get one free" pizza. Before the entire calamity, she had ordered two pizzas at the pizza place in this same complex. She said that it was just her and her husband and the baby at home and they really did not need two pizzas, so she offered the extra one to three fireman and a cop. We thanked her politely and waited until she was safely in her car. However, the empty pizza box was in the trash before she was out of the parking lot and we were looking for napkins to wipe our faces.

The cops like doughnuts and coffee, but keep a full pizza box away from a firefighter if you want to keep it full. When we returned to the fire hall, the assistant chief could not believe that we did not want a hot dog from the dozen or so left by the homecoming committee for our help. He thought that since we were not hungry, our call must have had a bad ending. Who among us was going to tell the chief that we were fifteen extra minutes on the call eating pizza before returning to the hall? The life expectancy of a pizza in a fire hall is measured in seconds. Oh well. The state statistics on how long the average emergency call takes will be only slightly askew.

After Glow

Psalm 34:17-18 says that when the righteous cry for help the Lord hears them. Well, that is just what happed to this lady in the Laundromat. She was frantic about her situation; however, she remained polite and maintained that she didn't know how the Lord was going to get her out of this one, but she knew He would. She apparently had called on Him many times in the past and her faith kept her spirits up during the ordeal. Later, the other two firemen said the good Lord was looking after her that day. Even in all of her troubles, she was witnessing to the rest of the people in the area. How true the words: the Lord works in mysterious ways.

CHAPTER 15

Fire Drills at the School

My sister, Charlene, or, as the family affectionately calls her, Charlie, is a nurse. While she was studying science in high school, I was a teacher on staff at the same school. This big city school had over two thousand students. Many people, including staff, did not know that Charlie was my sister, and we had to constantly explain the hugs, the flowers at homecoming, and the rides home in my car.

Because of the size of this school, the big city fire department made regular fire inspections of the building. They looked for faulty fire extinguishers and people parking in the fire lanes, and reviewed my fire drill logs.

One exercise of theirs was to come into the building through a back door (a fire door) and place a four-by-eight-foot sheet of plywood in an out-of-the-way hall or room. The plywood had a sign on it and a graphic of what looked like a trash can fire. The sign said "This is a test of a mock fire, report this to a school staff member immediately."

The fireman would then record the time it took for the report to get back to them. We looked pretty bad for several months of this testing. Our rules were so tight for student tardiness that sometimes it did take a while for the students to take the sign seriously.

A few years later, I became an assistant principal of this same school. The big city fire department members knew that I was a volunteer back in my little community a few miles away. Now that I had a little authority, I suggested that we write on the big board "Pull the nearest fire alarm when you see this sign." The students loved the opportunity to get outside for a few minutes and I got to count another fire drill to meet my annual quota required by law. I thought that may have been the reason I did not see the sign much after homecoming.

It was one of my sister's friends who told me the real reason. Apparently on Devil's Night, a few courageous students burned a small pile of fast food papers on the face of that sign. The sign was stored outside at the back of the parking lot of the fire department. The smudged sign had a note attached that said, "Call your local fire department if you see a fire near this sign." The fire department was sure that it was students who had defaced their sign. They could not prove their claim, but I told them I would at least be on the lookout for anyone talking about the problem. They sure did look at me funny while they were asking the questions. I sure am glad the culprits hadn't written, "Call your big city fire department," because there would have been suspicion to this day. They were an excellent fire department with many awards and I always envied their resources.

After Glow

Our Heavenly Father has used many signs throughout history to guide people and keep them out of danger. The big plywood sign was used as a warning sign for students and staff about the danger a fire could pose to a building with so many people inside. God used the sign of animal blood on door posts to save his followers. The rainbow is a sign, the Bethlehem star was a sign, and the list goes on.

God still uses signs in our lives. Sometimes those signs come through material that we read such as the Bible, sometimes they come through people who give you life-changing advice. I have always admired people who could listen and not insist on getting their own opinion expressed, especially when all you wanted was someone to listen so that you could figure out the problem yourself.

I have a friend, Ethel Elliott, who used to have this skill to listen. A lot of people have passed her way in her long ninety-nine-plus years of life. She is a non-threatening person who will tell you stories of the past that always reflect her faith. Her simple stories often *provide clear signs to the solutions to larger problems. She does not analyze or judge. She simply has so many of life's experiences to draw from that she always has an example. Her advice for a long life is, "Don't do things that you know you will regret, a clear conscience makes a long life." Talk about a sign!*

Listening and watching for a sign takes patience and occasionally a little time. Sometimes the sign is not what we had hoped for, but God's overall plan will be accomplished. Pray that you will be given wisdom and that the signs of our Heavenly Father will be made clear to you.

CHAPTER 16

The Four Seasons Family

Every small town has a family that just seems to struggle. They try to live life just like their neighbors. They take on projects just like everyone else, but these same projects always seem to end in disaster for them.

In one area of our town, there is a small subdivision of middle-class homes on lots that are fairly close together. The home are about twenty-five years old and some of the older folks were moving out as new, younger families were moving in. For most of these young families, this would be their first home. It was here that a stark example of one of these struggling families lived.

Even the most simple of projects often required that the fire department be called to their now-familiar address. Smoke and fire seemed to follow this family at the start of each new season of the year. During their first summer in their new home, they spent the day on the patio enjoying hamburgers on the grill while the kids played in the plastic pool at the end of the deck. After they had eaten their meal, Mrs. Disaster went into the house to get the dessert. As soon as she opened the door, she yelled, "Fire!" She ordered Mr. Disaster to go next door and call the fire department as she moved the kids to safety.

We arrived to find a smoke-filled structure and a family that was clear of the house. We hooked to a nearby fire hydrant and called for a backup truck. We then began our search for the source of the fire. After a quick inventory, we found that after Mr. Disaster had finished grilling the burgers and hot dogs, he turned the closed grill on high to burn food and grease off the grate. The problem was that he was doing this next to a window air conditioner intake which filled the house with the smoke.

In just a few short months, as fall arrived, Mrs. Disaster opened a basement window to air out a laundry room that contained a stinky sump pump crock. She left the window open and left to get a few groceries and laundry soap. Meanwhile, Mr. Disaster went to the back of the house to hook up a garden hose so he could wash windows. He was a cigar smoker and was not allowed to smoke in the house, so he took the opportunity to smoke while working outside. While hooking up the garden hose, he lost his stogie for moment in the dry leaves near the basement window. The light breeze of the day started some of the leaves smoldering. Mr. Disaster returned to the front of the house to continue his window cleaning. He opened a window, making a natural draft from the basement window into the living room. Mrs. Disaster returned home with the laundry soap and went downstairs toward the laundry room. She was about halfway to the washing machine when she yelled, "Fire!" So once again, we made our seasonal call.

A few months later, it was winter with just a few days remaining before the new year. Mr. and Mrs. Disaster, a working couple, decided to use the days off between Christmas and New Year to put away the Christmas decorations and get the house back to normal. After the Christmas tree was cleared of all the decorations, Mr. Disaster decided to ram the dry Christmas tree up into the fire place chimney from inside the house. Thinking he could make quick disposal of the tree, he lit the branches on fire. Apparently the previous owners had never cleaned the chimney of soot and the ivy growing around the chimney outside on the roof. When the chimney began to roar like a freight train, the Disasters decided to call us once again to put out the chimney fire. One of the firemen jokingly asked the Disasters if we could use their house as a training model in the spring.

The couple was always as good-natured about our visits as we were, and finally twelve months passed without a call. The story simply continued along a different avenue, however, as one of our volunteer firefighters, who was also a plumber, had the privilege of regular visits to the Disaster house. He said, "Remember the stinky sump pump crock? Well that was just the beginning!"

After Glow

It seems like Murphy's Law was founded on the principles by which the Disasters lived. They were by no means angry at the world for all of their troubles. On the contrary, they were a fun, humorous family that could laugh at misfortune and bounce right back for the next challenge that came their way. It is said that only you can allow the negative to influence your entire attitude. You can choose to see the overwhelming negative or the overpowering positive.

Matthew 6:27 asks us if all of our worries add a single moment to our lives. In fact, the opposite could add days to your life according to medical reports. Reading on in Matthew 6, we find that God has promised to take care of us as he does the gorgeous flowers of the woods and fields. They are more beautiful than Solomon in all his glory. Our Heavenly Father says those flowers will wither and die until next year. Don't you think He cares about you more than those flowers?

My daughter, Christy, is an excellent example of always being a cheerleader for the positive and downplaying the negative. She encourages herself and her students by giving thanks for the positive and

forgiving the negative. It has been her nature since childhood. A person will get so much more out of life when they can forgive and forget.

CHAPTER 17
The Goodfellows

As I mentioned earlier, the fire department does a lot of community service work. The subdivision picnic is just one of many annual projects. Our smoke alarm program for senior citizens is always well received. The medical tubes that are stored in the freezers of older people living alone are also popular. The tubes include copies of medication names, telephone numbers of family members and doctors, as well as other important information to be used by the police and fire if we found the person unconscious. Our dispatcher had the information as to who had one of our tubes and could relay that fact to us while we responded to a particular home. The freezer is also a good place to store important papers as the contents can usually withstand the heat of a fire.

The largest project was during December when we sold newspapers for the local Goodfellows organization. We sold the paper on street corners and at intersections to help raise money for the needy in the area. We got the names of folks who needed our help from a clearinghouse and the local paper donated several hundred papers for us to sell. The firemen put on their turnout gear, including boots and helmets, and hit the streets early on Saturday morning.

Christmas shoppers were our targets. We stood at busy intersections while the light changed and encourage a donation to the Goodfellows for a copy of the paper. It was great fun, with competition between fire stations as to who could raise the most money. Individual competitions were fierce as well.

Buck and I staked our claim on our favorite intersection year after year. We took a rookie with us one year so that we had three sides of the traffic light covered. The economy was doing well and the people were very generous. During low traffic times, we bantered with each other about how much money we had made and how a particular good-looking woman made some lewd comment to us. We had the rookie thinking that we blew a kiss to every flashy luxury car that had a woman driver. We told him we usually got five dollars from these folks rather than the usual one dollar for blowing the kiss.

We, of course, got the occasional old Scrooge that said a dollar was too much and he could buy the paper at the news stand for fifty cents. He just did not get the point that this was for the needy. Sometimes I wish we could collect good attitudes and hand them out to those kinds of folks who miss so much of life by being negative and self-centered.

As the papers began to run out, the rookie was really raking in the money. Buck and I were exploiting the luxury cars, but the rookie was working on the younger girls. They liked to see a young guy who looked tough in his fire gear. In fact, one car full of young girls heading for the mall pulled up alongside the rookie. The girls said, "To heck with your papers, we want you!" They pulled him into the car and we ran over to help him, but he sure wasn't putting up much of a fight. When one of the girls said to Buck, "Get out of here, old man!" (he was over forty) I thought Buck was going to get sick sucking in his gut and sticking out his chest. He even picked the rookie up out of the car with one arm to show off his strength. To Buck's credit, one of the girls did say that for an old guy he was rather cute. He asked me what I thought of that. I told him I would rather be young and ugly.

After Glow

Being part of a service organization or volunteering in community- and church-sponsored missions and other outreach programs is very rewarding. The people who are drawn to such activities provide a wonderful opportunity to expand our circle of friends. The goodwill and satisfaction experienced cannot be measured. When you see the good that the benefactors receive from the work these organizations provide, it is uplifting and often life-changing.

Matthew 25:34-40 is an incentive like none other. God tells us in these verses that when we help our brothers and sisters in need, we are helping God. Lifting up others who may be struggling has a way of lifting everyone's self worth, no matter which end of the spectrum we happen to be on.

Postscript

I cannot end this little book without expressing my appreciation for the hard work firefighters do every day. Having been there, I understand the dedication necessary to do the job well. Even though my department had a lot of fun while doing its job, I cannot express how special the people are who make up a local fire department. They care about people and that is why they do what they do. If you look into their eyes, you will see that little sparkle that shows that it was not just my department that had these mishaps. They all have their own smoke stories about their families and friends in the fire service.

When you see firefighters raising money for a cause, please support them. The money that the car wash or pancake supper is providing is going toward a new truck to protect your family or help a neighbor in need. I have been a soldier, schoolteacher and administrator, city councilman, and firefighter. Each job has had its own unique opportunity to help others, but my experience has been that people always appreciated the job of a firefighter the most.

Thank you for purchasing this book. I hope it has provided you with a small sample of the work of a local fire department along with a little fun and enjoyable reading with a message of hope as well.

Fire Safety Information

(Reprinted courtesy of the United States Fire Administration)

Working Together for Home Fire Safety

More than 4,000 Americans die each year in fires and approximately 20,000 are injured. An overwhelming number of fires occur in the home. There are time-tested ways to prevent and survive a fire. It's not a question of luck. It's a matter of planning ahead.

Every Home Should Have at Least One Working Smoke Alarm

Buy a smoke alarm at any hardware or discount store. It's inexpensive protection for you and your family. Install a smoke alarm on every level of your home. A working smoke alarm can double your chances of survival. Test it monthly, keep it free of dust, and replace the battery at least once a year. Smoke alarms themselves should be replaced after ten years of service, or as recommended by the manufacturer.

Prevent Electrical Fires

Never overload circuits or extension cords. Do not place cords and wires under rugs, over nails, or in high-traffic areas. Immediately shut off and unplug appliances that sputter, spark, or emit an unusual smell. Have them professionally repaired or replaced.

Use Appliances Wisely

When using appliances follow the manufacturer's safety precautions. Overheating, unusual smells, shorts, and sparks are all warning signs that appliances need to be shut off, then replaced or repaired. Unplug appliances when not in use. Use safety caps to cover all unused outlets, especially if there are small children in the home.

Alternate Heaters

Portable heaters need their space. Keep anything combustible at least three feet away.

Keep fire in the fireplace. Use fire screens and have your chimney cleaned annually. The creosote buildup can ignite a chimney fire that could easily spread.

Kerosene heaters should be used only where approved by authorities. Never use gasoline or camp-stove fuel. Refuel outside and only after the heater has cooled.

Affordable Home Fire Safety Sprinklers

When home fire sprinklers are used with working smoke alarms, your chances of surviving a fire are greatly increased. Sprinklers are affordable - they can increase property value and lower insurance rates.

Plan Your Escape

Practice an escape plan from every room in the house. Caution everyone to stay low to the floor when escaping from fire and never to open doors that are hot. Select a location where everyone can meet after escaping the house. Get out first, then call for help.

Caring for Children

Children under five are naturally curious about fire. Many play with matches and lighters. Tragically, children set over 20,000 house fires every year. Take the mystery out of fire play by teaching your children that fire is a tool, not a toy.

Caring for Older People

Every year over 1,200 senior citizens die in fires. Many of these fire deaths could have been prevented. Seniors are especially vulnerable because many live alone and can't respond quickly.

Escape Planning

Of the 4,000 deaths and 20,000 injuries resulting from fire, those due to failed emergency escapes are particularly avoidable.

The United States Fire Administration (USFA) believes that having a sound escape plan will greatly reduce fire deaths and protect you and your family's safety if a fire occurs.

Have a Sound Fire Escape Plan

In the event of a fire, remember - time is the biggest enemy and every second counts! Escape plans help you get out of your home quickly. In less than thirty seconds a small flame can get completely out of control and turn into a major fire. It only takes minutes for a house to fill with thick black smoke and become engulfed in flames.

Special Considerations

Practice Escaping From Every Room In The Home

Practice escape plans every month. The best plans have two ways to get out of each room. If the primary way is blocked by fire or smoke, you will need a second way out. A secondary route might be a window onto an adjacent roof or using an Underwriter's Laboratory (UL) listed collapsible ladder for escape from upper story windows. Make sure that windows are not stuck, screens can be taken out quickly and that security bars can be properly opened. Also, practice feeling your way out of the house in the dark or with your eyes closed.

Security Bars Require Special Precautions

Security bars may help to keep your family safe from intruders, but they can also trap you in a deadly fire! Windows and doors with security bars must have quick release devices to allow them to be opened immediately in an emergency. Make sure everyone in the family understands and practices how to properly operate and open locked or barred doors and windows.

Immediately Leave The Home

When a fire occurs, do not waste any time saving property. Take the safest exit route, but if you must escape through smoke, remember to crawl low, under the smoke and keep your mouth covered. The smoke contains toxic gases which can disorient you or, at worst, overcome you.

Never Open Doors That Are Hot To The Touch

When you come to a closed door, use the back of your hand to feel the top of the door, the doorknob, and the crack between the door and door frame to make sure that fire is not on the other side. If it feels hot, use your secondary escape route. Even if the door feels cool, open it carefully. Brace your shoulder against the door and open it slowly. If heat and smoke come in, slam the door and make sure it is securely closed, then use your alternate escape route.

Designate A Meeting Place Outside and Take Attendance

Designate a meeting location away from the home, but not necessarily across the street. For example, meet under a specific tree or at the end of the driveway or front sidewalk to make sure everyone has gotten out safely and no one will be hurt looking for someone who is already safe. Designate one person to go to a neighbor's home to phone the fire department.

Once Out, Stay Out

Remember to escape first, then notify the fire department using the 911 system or proper local emergency number in your area. Never go back into a burning building for any reason. Teach children not to hide from firefighters. If someone is missing, tell the firefighters. They are equipped to perform rescues safely.

Mike Davis was born in southeast Michigan. He was raised in a Christian home with three siblings. As a family they were brought up to appreciate the value of money and respect for hard work. He was a soldier, teacher, school administrator, volunteer firefighter, and city councilman. He sincerely believes that, of all the jobs and responsibilities he has had the pleasure of experiencing, the work as a firefighter was the experience that was most appreciated by others. Mike lives with his wife June in the Upper Peninsula of Michigan near their two children and two grandchildren.

Smoke Stories: Tales of a Volunteer Firefighter

Please send me (quantity) _____ at $9.95 each

Name: _____

Address: _____

City, State, Zip: _____

Phone: _____

E-mail: _____

Total (number of books x $9.95) _____

Shipping: ($3.00 plus $1.00 per book) _____

Subtotal: _____

Michigan sales tax (6%) _____

TOTAL DUE: _____

Make checks payable to Mike Davis.

Mail this completed form (or a copy) along with your check to:

Mike Davis

3349 E. Rocky Trail

Cedarville, MI 49719